AF539190

Preface

The rapid increase in global warming would result in long term changes in climate condition of world. The economics of environmental pollution depletion and degradation of resources has in fact been neglected as compared to the issues of growth and expansion.

Life survives on the planet earth due to energy from Sun, which is the only source of energy in the universe. About 30 per cent of the Sun light that beams towards earth is deflected by the outer atmosphere and scattered back to the space and the rest reaches the planet surface and is again reflected upwards as a slow moving energy called as Infra-red radiation and is absorbed by the water vapour, carbon dioxide, ozone and methane which ultimately slows its escape from the atmosphere. Due to rapid urbanization, huge automobile transportations, industrialization and increase of population of living society day-by-day, the original purity of the constituents of the environment become impure and poisoned by inter mixing of domestic garbage and wastes, drain water, industrial wastes, chemical effluents, smoke, solids and gases and automobile exhausts etc. the decrease of the purity of all constituents of the environment is called environmental pollution. To live healthy, peacefully, stress free, it need due consideration for pollution free environment society. This book is very much helpful to planners, scholars, engineers and others in particular and all human beings in general.

Dr. Rabi N. Misra

Acknowledgements

I am thankful to all paper contributors of this book. It is not possible in my part to edit this book without their active co-operation and help.

My wife Smt. Swarna Prava Misra has taken all positive steps for writing this book. My son Roopesh, Rookesh along with my daughter-in-laws Amrita and Bandita were taken all the pain for writing this book.

I convey my thanks and express gratitude to Mr. Tilak Wasan, the Director/Owner cf Discovery Publishing House Pvt. Ltd., New Delhi for publishing this book without any hesitation. I am also thankful to his son Mr. Parul Wasan and other members and staff of Discovery Publishing House Pvt. Ltd. for their kind help and co-operation in publishing the book in time.

I am very much thankful to the President of SAURAVA (An Environment Protection and Pollutions Control Unit, Berhampur, Odisha) Smt. Swarna Prava Misra for conducting a National Seminar at Berhampur and her kind co-operation in editing this book.

Dr. Rabi N. Misra

Contents

India 2025—Environment

G. Chandrayya
Selection Grade Lecturer in Commerce
Government College (A), Rajahmundry

Dr. R.N. Misra
Visiting Professor, Department of Commerce and Management Studies, Government College (A), Rajahmundry

Introduction

The rapid increase in population and economic development has led to severe environmental degradation that undermines the environmental resource base upon which sustainable development depends. The economics of environmental pollution, depletion and degradation of resources has in fact been neglected as compared to the issues of growth and expansion. India has been no exception to this worldwide phenomenon, rather the trends of environmental deterioration in India, because of the substantial increase in its population, have been far more prominent as compared to other developing economies.

The country has indeed made substantial progress in most indicators of human development since Independence when it was predominantly an agrarian economy with a stagnant national income. Encouraging achievements have been recorded in the age-specific mortality rates; expectation of life at birth; and aspects related to livelihood conditions like education, nutritional security and health. With the country's population having grown three-fold and the urban population itself quadrupling in four decades (1951-1991), the current infrastructure in most of the cases is not only over stretched but also inadequate. With a population of over a billion, India supports 16 per cent of the world's population on 2.4 per cent of the world's land resulting in a paucity of resources that jeopardises growth in the longer run.

Urban development in India is presently going through a very dynamic stage, the percentage of population in urban centres itself having increased from 14 per cent in the 1940s to about 33 per cent in 2000. The unprecedented challenge of such an urban shift has resulted in Indian cities degenerating into slums and squatters camps. The rapid expansion of cities has brought to the fore acute problems of transport congestion, atmospheric pollution and unwise water and solid waste management resulting in the degradation of the quality of life. The deterioration of environmental quality in Indian cities is but one aspect of the threat to the quality of life, the other perhaps more pertinent issue being that of the sustainability of growth itself.

The much needed impetus to industrial development has resulted in huge residuals, having undesirable effects on the environment—air, water and land, disproportional to their contribution to overall economic growth. For instance, the iron and steel industry contributes 55 per cent of the particulate matter load while adding 16 per cent to the total industrial output. The industrial BOD load from chemicals and food processing industries is as much as 86 per cent against the industry's contribution of 25 per cent to the total industrial output.

These unsustainable growth trends increase the vulnerability of the economically weaker sections to environmental degradation and pollution, on account of their direct dependence on natural resources like land, forests and various common property sources for fuelwood, fodder, and water. In the absence of alternatives, the imbalanced competition for natural resources could significantly contribute to weakening the support base of the poor further and perpetuating poverty and a poor quality of life. Hence for a developing country like India, the key to poverty elimination is the country's ability to regenerate its environment and assist its masses to retain control over their living conditions.

Based on studies done at TERI (Tata Energy Research Institute)—Looking Back to Think Ahead (TERI 1998; DISHA (Directions, Innovations and Strategies for Harnessing Actions for Sustainable Development) and State of Environment—India this chapter aims to highlight the key environmental concerns that have emerged in the country. Section 1 focuses on the prevalent status and causal factors of the major environmental concerns such as air, water resources and pollution, solid waste management and also touches briefly on the issues of land degradation and biodiversity. Baseline scenarios have been developed on how these trends are likely to unfold by the year 2025, considering the base year as 1997. Section 2 puts forward the strategies for a reform agenda that is more widespread and proposes its implementation at a considerably quicker pace. Alternative case projections for the year 2025 are presented accordingly, assuming that the proposed strategies are implemented in full within a well-defined time frame.

Growing Environmental Concerns—Compulsions of Economic Development

This section focuses on the prevailing environmental concerns and the root causes of the degrading environment emphasising current effects on resource depletion and environmental degradation currently and expected future trends. Projections have been made as per BAU (business-as-usual) scenario for the year 2025 in view of the current socio-economic, policy and technological factors prevalent in India.

Air Pollution

Air pollution in India has been aggravated over the years by developments that typically occur as economies become industrialised: growing cities, increasing traffic, rapid economic development and industrialisation and higher levels of energy consumption. In India, air pollution is restricted mostly to urban areas, where automobiles are the major contributors and to a few other areas with a concentration of industries and thermal power plants. The major sources of air pollution in the country are industries (toxic gases), thermal power plants (fly ash and sulphur dioxide), and motor vehicles (carbon monoxide, particulate matter, hydrocarbons and oxides of nitrogen). Major polluting industries and automobiles emit tonnes of pollutants every day, putting citizens, at great health risk. The national capital—Delhi, is already among the most polluted cities in the world.

The incidence of respiratory diseases in most of the major cities in India has also increased considerably over the years. In a study of 2031 children and adults in five major cities of India, of the 1852 children tested, 51.4 per cent had levels of lead in their blood above 10 µg/dl. The percentage of children having 10 µg/dl or higher lead levels ranged from 39.9 per cent in Bangalore to 61.8 per cent in Mumbai. Among the adults, 40.2 per cent had lead levels of about 10 fig/dl

Box 1 below lists the principal sources and environmental effects of some of the major air pollutants.

Box 1. Principal Sources and Environmental Effects of Selected Atmospheric Pollutants

Pollutant	Principal sources related to human activity	Effects	Remarks
Carbon monoxide	Incomplete fuel combustion as in motor vehicles)	Deprives tissues of oxygen. People with cardio-respiratory diseases more sensitive.	CO is one of the most widely distributed of all air pollutants—global emissions of all other major air pollutants. Contribution of natural sources is small. The largest source is petrol-driven motor vehicles.
Sulphur dioxide	Burning of sulphur-containing fuels like coal and oil	Combined with smoke, increases risk and effects of respiratory diseases. Causes suffocation and irritation of throat and eyes. Combines with atmospheric water vapour to produce acid rain. Leads to acidification of lakes and soils. Corrodes buildings.	
Suspended particulate matter	Smoke from domestic, industrial and vehicular sources	Possible toxic effects depend on specific composition. Aggravates effects of sulphur dioxide. Reduces sunlight and visibility. Increases corrosion.	Chemically, a most diverse group of substances. Natural sources include dust-storms and volcanic eruptions.
Oxides of nitrogen	Fuel combustion in motor vehicles, power stations, and furnaces	Possible increase in acute respiratory' infections and bronchitis morbidity in children. Produce brown haze in city air. Causes corrosion.	Combustion oxidizes both the nitrogen in the fuel and some of the nitrogen present in the air. producing several oxides of nitrogen. However, only NO and NO_2 are known to have adverse environmental or biological effects.

...(Contd.)

Volatile hydrocarbons	Partial combustion of carbonaceous fuels, industrial processes, disposal of solid wastes.	React with other pollutants to produce eye irritants (acroiein. aldehydes). Ethylene is harmful to plants. Aerosol panicles reduce visibility. May produce unpleasant odours.	
Oxidants and ozone	Emissions from motor vehicles. Photochemical reactions of nitrogen oxides and reactive hydrocarbons.	Cause eyes irritation and impaired pulmonary function in diseased persons. Corrode materials and reduces visibility. Ozone is one of the most damaging pollutants for plants.	Mainly derivative: products of atmospheric reactions between other pollutants. Ozone is a natural and essential constituent of the upper atmosphere.
Lead	Main source is emission from motor vehicles. Other sources include smelting and refining lead, producing batteries, paints, etc.	Adversely affects blood and human nervous system. Causes anaemia, brain dysfunctions and kidney damage.	Alkyl lead, used as an anti-knock agent in petrol, is released into the atmosphere as fine particles when petrol is bumt.

Sources: United Nationals Environment Programme (1991), Centre for Science and Environment (1982)

Vehicular Pollution

Vehicular emission is the major contributor to the rising levels of all major pollutants. It is an issue of prime concern since these emissions are from ground level sources and thus have the greatest impact on the health of the population exposed to it. The increase in the number of vehicles contributes significantly to the total air pollution load in many urban areas. The number of motor vehicles in India has increased from 0.3 million in 1951 to 40.94 million in 1998. CO (Carbon monoxide) and HC (hydrocarbons) respectively account for 64 per cent and 23 per cent of the total emission load due to vehicles in all cities considered together. Table 1.1 highlights the types of pollutants from different sectors in Delhi and reflects the significant share of the transport sector in the same.

Table 1.1 : Sectoral Contribution to Emissions in Delhi (tonnes/day)

Pollutant	Transport	Power	Industries	Domestic	Total
TSP	13 (10%)	50 (37%)	60 (44%)	12 (9%)	138
SO_2	11 (6%)	121 (68%)	35 (20%)	12 (6%)	179
NO_x	157 (49%)	143 (44%)	20 (6%)	3 (1%)	323
HC	810 (76%)	8 (1%)	128 (12%)	117 (11%)	1063
CO	310	2(<1%)	6 (2%)	2(<1%)	320
	(97%)				

Source: CPCB 1995.

Apart from the concentration of vehicles in urban areas, other reasons for increasing vehicular pollution include the types of engines used, age of vehicles, poor road conditions, outdated automotive technologies, poor fuel quality and traffic congestion resulting from clumsy traffic management systems.

Air Quality Profile

In order to determine the air quality status and trends, assess health hazards, disseminate air quality data, and to control and regulate pollution, the CPCB (Central Pollution Control Board) initiated a nationwide framework of NAAQM (National Ambient Air Quality Monitoring) in 1984 with 28 stations at 7 cities. Presently, the network has 290 monitoring stations in 92 cities and towns throughout the country. The pollutants being monitored are mainly SPM (suspended particulate matter), SO_2 (sulphur dioxide) and NO_X oxides of nitrogen. SPM is one of the most critical pollutants in terms of its impact on air quality and is also the most common pollutant across all sectors. The ranges of SPM concentration (annual average) in the major metropolitan cities in India are shown in Table 1.2.

Table 1.2 : Range of Annual Averages of SPM in Major Indian Cities

Sl. No.	City	Area land use	Range of annual average of SPM (μg/m³) 1990-98 Minimum	Maximum	Mean of annual averages (μg/m³)
1.	Delhi	Residential	300	409	355
		Industrial	314	431	381
2.	Mumbai	Residential	196	327	230
		Industrial	150	276	224
3.	Kolkata	Residential	205	491	327
		Industrial	286	640	434
4.	Chennai	Residential	72	118	99
		Industrial	53	147	123
5.	Bengaluru	Residential	60	239	158
		Industrial	99	153	125
6.	Ahmedabad	Residential	198	316	261
		Industrial	201	306	243
7.	Hyderabad	Residential	135	184	158
		Industrial	72	259	153

Source: CPCB 2000a

As against to the maximum permissible limits laid down by CPCB for annual average concentration of SPM in ambient air - 70 μg/m³ in sensitive areas, 140 μg/m³ in residential areas and 360 μg/m³ in industrial areas, it is clearly evident that the SPM levels are high in most of the metropolitan cities in India.

Projections for Integrated Air Pollution Loads—BAU (Business as Usual) Scenario

The future scenario of air pollution in India has been calculated considering the integrated impact from major contributing sectors, *i.e.,* domestic, transport, manufacturing industries and power. In the absence of a comprehensive emission inventory, projections have been made only for SPM, which is the most common pollutant across all sectors and is critical for air quality in many cities.

- Emissions from the transport sector have been calculated based on projections for a count of vehicles, in line with the projections for growth in population and economic activity.
- Air pollution from the manufacturing sector has been worked out on the basis of emission load per unit of output for some of the resource intensive and highly polluting industries-copper, aluminium, steel, cement, fertilisers, textiles and PVC (poly-vinyl chloride).
- Projections for pollutant loads from power generation have been arrived at, considering a continued reliance of the power sector on coal-based generation, resulting a higher SPM load. It is further assumed that all coal-based power plants will have installed ESPs (electro-static precipitators) to limit SPM emissions.
- The SPM contribution of the domestic sector takes into account a shift towards cleaner gaseous fuel and fewer emissions from the residential sector.

Figure 1.1 highlights the projections for the pollutant load generated from each of the sectors.

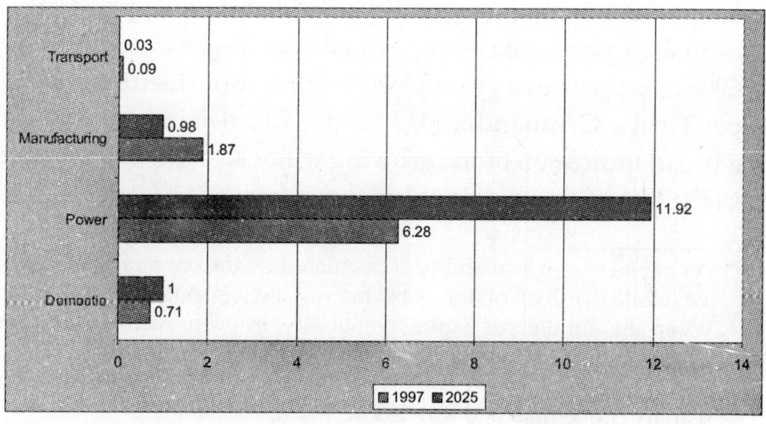

Fig. 1.1 : Pollutant loads generated (BAU scenario) (million tonnes)

Projections indicate that the overall SPM load is likely to get reduced in the time frame 1997-2025 at around 2 per cent per annum, although a bulk of the load would continue to emanate from power generation (66% in 2025). The drop in pollution loads from the domestic sector is on account of a likely shift to commercial fuels in rural India.

Water

Water Resources

India receives an average annual rainfall equivalent of about 4000 cubic kilometres. This is unevenly distributed across different parts of the country and most of the rainfall is confined to the monsoon season, from June to September. Thus, while India is considered to be rich in terms of annual rainfall and total water resources, water is spatially and temporally very unevenly distributed. Based on per capita water availability,[1] some river basins fall in the category of water scarce[2] and water stressed regions, and several others suffer from absolute scarcity. Though water resource availability is estimated to be 1085.9 billion cubic metres, annual average utilisable per capita water resources vary considerably from as high as 3020 in the Narmada basin to as low as about 180 cubic metres and less in the Sabarmati basin, as against a desired availability of 1700 per capita per year. The estimated per capita water availability has also declined from 6008 cubic metres a year in 1947 to 2266 cubic metres in 1997, as per TERI's 'Green India 2047' study. This declining figure gives a broad indication of the growing water scarcity in the country in the last fifty years since Independence.

---

1 Per capita water availability is calculated on the basis of total resource availability of 1085 billion cubic metres and a population of 1 billion

2 When the annual per capita availability, in cubic metres, falls below 1700, it is held to be a situation of water stress, availability of less than 1000 is labelled as water scarcity, and of less than 500 is termed absolute scarcity (Engelman and Roy 1993).

The growing gap between demand and supply has led to overdevelopment of groundwater, making its overuse emerge as a major concern in a few states. Against a critical level of 80 per cent, the level of exploitation is over 98 per cent in Punjab and about 80 per cent in Haryana. The problem is also becoming increasingly serious in Tamil Nadu, where the level of exploitation exceeds 60 per cent and in Rajasthan, where it is 53 per cent. Between 1984/85 and 1994/95, the number of dark blocks with groundwater exploitation greater than 85 per cent increased on an average by over threefold in a few states (Table 1.3).

Table 1.3 : Blocks with intensive exploitation of groundwater (utilization exceeds 85% of the annual utilisable potential)

	% of blocks using ground-water intensively	
State	**1984/85**	**1994/95**
Gujarat	3	25
Punjab	54	62
Rajasthan	9	29
Tamil Nadu	14	26

Source : Saleth 1996.

Water Pollution

The problem of fresh water pollution in India came to the forefront towards the beginning of 1970s with the domestic sewage and industrial waste discharges being the most critical sources of pollution in cities. This resulted in the promulgation of the Water (Prevention and Control of Pollution) Act, 1974 and establishment of the National Water Quality Network in 1979. The sources of water pollution include point and non-point sources like discharges from industries and storm water respectively. While pollution from point sources can be controlled, it is difficult to control pollution from non-point sources such as agriculture run-off, leaching from waste disposal sites and storm water.

The total wastewater generation from domestic sources in class I towns is 16.27 billion litres and of this a mere 25 per cent is treated. The increase in treatment capacities have also not shown a commensurate increase as the share of waste water which is untreated and disposed into our surface water bodies, has increased from 61 per cent in 1978-79 to 76 per cent in 1994-95.

Water pollution, in the industrial sector is concentrated within a few subsectors mainly in the form of toxic wastes and organic pollutants. Of the total pollution load generated by industrial subsectors, 40%-45% is contributed by the processing of industrial chemicals. In terms of the total organic pollution, expressed as BOD, nearly 40 per cent arises from the food industries followed by industrial chemicals and the pulp and paper industry. Other major sector of concern is that of small-scale industries with more than 2 million units where pollution abatement has been neglected so far. Depending on the traditional crafts and culture of the area, small-scale industries like chemical, textiles, food processing and tanneries are found in large clusters in different states. States with over a lakh registered small-scale industries include Andhra Pradesh, Gujarat, Madhya Pradesh, Punjab. Tamil Nadu, Uttar Pradesh, and West Bengal. Of these very few of the clusters have opted for CETPs (Common Effluent Treatment Plants) to control water pollution but most of these CETPs either do not function at all or do not treat effluents to the desired quality.

Presently the institutional mechanisms to address pollution in the agriculture sector are also missing, as the sector is out of the ambit of the pollution control boards. The problem is acute in the riparian states of Punjab, Haryana, Uttar Pradesh and Tamil Nadu. Excessive use of fertilizers has led to an increase in the levels of nitrates in the shallow groundwater sources. The nitrate content of well water in a few districts of Uttar Pradesh, Haryana, and Punjab is far beyond the standard prescribed safe limit of 45 mg/litre. Severe degradation of ground water sources is also resulting from dumped solid wastes and human waste in dug wells.

Water Quality Profile

Pressures due to inadequate collection and inefficient treatment of domestic wastewater, discharge of highly complex wastes from industries and the polluted runoff from agricultural fields, have resulted in considerable degradation in the quality of water sources. Indicators of this deterioration include depletion of oxygen, excessive presence of pathogens, settling of suspended material during lean flow conditions and bad odour.

The quality of river water is monitored at 480 stations under different programmes such as MINARS (monitoring of Indian national aquatic resources), GEMS (global environmental monitoring systems), and GAP (ganga action plan). A number of physical, chemical, biological and bacteriological parameters are being measured under the programme, but the important ones include BOD (biochemical oxygen demand), DO (dissolved oxygen), and TC (total coliform) count. Heavy metals are however not included under the monitoring programme. Some of the polluted river stretches, their critical parameters and possible sources of pollution are listed in the Table 1.4 below.

Table 1.4 : List of Polluted River Stretches

River	Polluted stretch	Desired class	Existing class	Critical para-meters	Possible source of pollution
Sabarmati	Immediate upsteam of Ahmedabad up to Sabarmati Ashram	B	E	DO, BOD, Coliform	Domestic and industrial waste from Ahmedabad
	Sabarmati Ashram to Vautha	D	E	DO, BOD, Coliform	Domestic and industrial waste from Ahmedabad
Submarekha	Hatia dam to Bhargora	C	D/E	-do-	Domestic and industrial waste from Ranchi and Jamshedpur

...(*Contd.*)

Godavari	Downstream of Nasik and Nanded	C	D/E	BOD	Wastes from sugar industries, distilleries and food processing industries
Krishna	Karad to Sangli	C	D/E	BOD	Wastes from sugar industries and distilleries
Sutlej	Downstream of Ludhiana to Haike	C	D/E	DO, BOD	Industrial wastes from hosieries, tanneries, electro-plating and engineering industries and domestic waste from Ludhiana and Jalandhar
	Downstream of Nangal	C	D/E	Ammonia	Wastes from fertilizer and chloralkali mills from Nangal
Yamuna	Delhi to confluence with Chambal	C	D/E	DO, BOD, Coliform	Domestic and industrial wastes from Delhi, Mathura and Agra
	In the city limits of Delhi, Mathura and Agra	B	D/E	DO, BOD, Coliform	Domestic and industrial wastes from Delhi, Mathura and Agra
Hindon	Saharanpur to confluence with yamuna	C	D	DO, BOD, Coliform	Industrial and domestic wastes from Saharanpur and Ghaziabad
Chambal	Downstream of Nagda and downstream of Kota	C	D/E	BOD, DO	Domestic and industrial waste from Nagda and Kota

...(*Contd.*)

Damodar	Downstream of Dhanbad	C	D/E	BOD, Toxicity	Industrial wastes from Dhanbad, Durgapur, Asansol, Haldia and Burnpur
Gomati	Lucknow to confluence with Ganges	C	D/E	DO, BOD, Coliform	Industrial wastes from distilleries and domestic wastes from Lucknow
Kali	Downstream of Modinagar to confluence with Ganges	C	D/E	BOD, Coliform	Industrial and domestic wastes from Modinagar

Source : CPCB 1999.

"Water quality and the desired water quality is expressed in classes A, B, C, D, and E, which reflect the best use of that water. Class A indicates that water is fit for drinking without conventional treatment but after disinfection; Class B that it is suitable for outdoor bathing; and Class C, that it is suitable for drinking after conventional treatment. Class D water is suitable for propagation of wildlife and fisheries and Class E water can be used for irrigation, industrial cooling, and controlled waste disposal.

Projections for Water Requirements—BAU Scenario

Demand for fresh water will continue to grow from all sectors, due to additional requirements from agriculture and increased migration to urban areas. To project the water requirement by the year 2025 under a baseline scenario, four major water-consuming sectors have been considered and the cumulative water requirement has been estimated based on:

- *Agricultural* cropping intensity of 157 per cent with 60 per cent of the gross cropped area under irrigation.
- Per capita *domestic* supply of 135 litres a day in the urban areas and 40 litres per day in rural areas.
- An estimated 3 per cent increase in water consumption by the *industrial sector* in line with the projections for growth in economic activity.

- Projections for water requirements in *the power sector* assume an increase in dry collection practices and better process operations for fly ash collection and steam generation respectively.

Based on the above, total water demand under the BAU scenario is as Table 1.5.

Table 1.5 : Total Water Demand Projections: Base Case (billion cubic metres)

Year	Irrigation	Domestic	Manufacturing	Power	Total
1997	528.85	23.52	1.6	1.39	555.36
2025	789.50	39.76	4.79	3.75	837.80

These projections for water demand when compared to the estimated availability of 1085.9 billion cubic metres indicate an overall net marginal positive balance of only 248.1 billion cubic metres by the year 2025. However, given the uneven distribution of the resource, as discussed, it is projected that the country will go, from the present state of water stress, to a state of water scarcity, with an average annual per capita availability of 750 cubic metres by 2025. Further, due to wide inequality ia the consumption patterns of different sectors, competition for water from different sectors may trigger disputes among these sectors as well.

Projections for Water Pollution Loads – BAU Scenario

The current state of infrastructure marked with inadequate collection networks and treatment capacities forces discharge of untreated or partly treated waste water into natural drains joining the rivers, lakes, and sea. The polluted rivers and other water bodies is a direct consequence of the inadequate level of collection and treatment in Indian cities.

BOD projections from the urban domestic sector assume an overall wastewater collection efficiency of about 70 per cent in 2025. It is also assumed that all production units would have facilities to control pollution in accordance with the CPCB's year wise analysis of the polluting units and strict compliance due to stringent environmental regulations. The estimated pollutant load, in terms of BOD, from the untreated wastewater from the domestic sector (urban and rural areas) and industrial sector under the base case is presented in Figure 1.2.

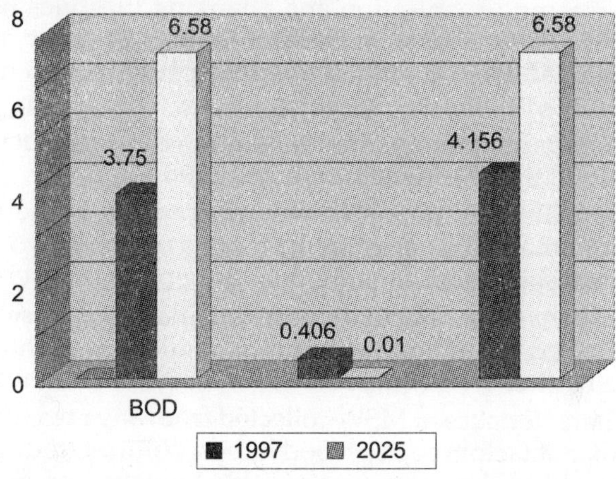

Fig. 1.2 : BOD projections (BAU scenario) (million tonnes)

Annual discharge of the order of 6.58 million tonnes from the domestic sector, as projected is beyond the self-cleansing capacity of the water bodies, rendering them unfit for several beneficial uses.

Solid Waste Management

Municipal Solid Waste

The growth in MSW (municipal solid waste) generation in India has outpaced the growth in population in the recent years. The daily per capita generation of municipal solid waste in India ranges from about 100 g in small towns to 500 g in large towns. The recyclable content of waste ranges from 13 per cent to 20 per cent. The survey conducted by CPCB puts total municipal waste generation from Class I and II cities to around 18 million tonnes in 1997. The reason for this escalating trend is a mix of the changing lifestyles, food habits and changes in standard of living.

The TERI "Green India 2047' study made the following observations on the situation of municipal solid waste management in the country:

- increasing urbanisation and changing lifestyles has led to, the solid waste generated in Indian cities having increased from 6 million tonnes in 1947 to 47.8 million tonnes in 1997.
- The production and consumption of plastic increased over 70 times between 1960 and 1995.
- The collection of municipal solid waste is inefficient (more than 25 per cent of the total is not collected at all), its transport is inadequate, and its disposal is unscientific.
- More than one-fourth of the municipal solid waste is not collected at all, and the landfills to dispose of the waste are neither well equipped nor managed efficiently.

The characteristics of MSW collected from any area depends on a number of factors such as food habits, cultural traditions of inhabitants, lifestyles, climate, etc. Table 1.6 below presents the changes in the characteristics of waste in past two decades. The changes in the relative shares of different constituents of waste in the past several decades, as shown by the data, can be attributed largely to changing lifestyles and increasing consumerism.

Table 1.6 : Physico-chemical Characteristics of MSW

Component	% of wet weight	
	1971-73* (40 cities)	1995** (23 cities)
Paper	4.14	5.78
Plastics	0.69	3.90
Metals	0.50	1.90
Glass	0.40	2.10
Rags	3.83	3.50
Ash and fine earth	49.20	40.30
Total compostable matter	41.24	41.80
Calorific value (kcal/kg)	800-1100	<1500
Carbon-nitrogen ratio	20-30	25-40

Source: *Bhide and Sundaresan 1983, **EPTRI 1995

Disposal of waste is a major issue of concern in India. Respective municipalities collect MSW in cities and transport it to the designated disposal sites, which is normally a low-lying area on the outskirts of a city. The choice of a disposal site is more a matter of what is available than what is suitable. Only a few cities follow good practices such as organized dumping of wastes, using mechanized equipment for levelling and compacting the wastes, and covering the top layer with earth before compacting it further. Of late, some cities have also started to practice composting the organic fraction of waste.

Management of biomedical waste is another issue of concern for municipalities. This, waste produced in hospitals generally has high contamination of pathogens, making it hazardous. It also includes scalpels, needles, bandages, and other wastes from operating theatres and laboratories as well as infectious items, e.g. amputated body-parts, body fluids, cultures of contagious viruses, excreta from patients with highly contagious diseases, etc. Though waste from hospitals and nursing homes are required to be collected and treated separately, in most cities and towns such waste continues to form a part of the MSW in absence of any dedicated disposal facilities for hospital waste. The MoEF, Government of India has issued the Municipal Solid Wastes (management and handling) Rules in the year 2000, which identify the CPCB (Central Pollution Control Board) as the agency to monitor the implementation of these rules. For the management of bio-medical waste, the MoEF has notified Bio-Medical Waste (management and handling) Rules in 1998 under sections 6, 8 and 25 of the Environment (Protection) Act of 1986.

Industrial Solid Waste

Industries can be broadly classified into those that produce non-hazardous waste and those that produce hazardous waste. Non-hazardous waste can be either biodegradable or non-biodegradable. The major industries in urban areas that generate substantial amounts of biodegradable solid waste are fruit processing, cotton mills, paper mills, sugar mills, and textile factories. The major generators of non-biodegradable industrial solid waste are thermal power plants producing coal ash, integrated iron and steel mills producing blast furnace slag and steel melting slag, such non-ferrous industries as aluminum, zinc, and copper, which produce red mud and tailings, and fertilizer and allied industries which produce gypsum.

Some of the wastes generated by industries are deemed to be hazardous wastes because they contain substances that are toxic to plants and animals or are flammable, corrosive, explosive or highly reactive, chemically. Box 2 lists the categories of hazardous waste as specified under the Hazardous Wastes (management and handling) Rules.

Box 2. Types of Hazardous Waste

Waste Category Nos.	Types of Waste
No. 1	Cyanide waste
No. 2	Metal finishing, waste
No. 3	Waste containing water soluble chemical compounds of lead, copper, zinc, chromium, nickel, selenium, barium and antimony
No. 4	Mercury, Arsenic, Thallium and Cadmium-bearing wastes
No. 5	Non-halogenated hydrocarbons including solvents
No. 6	Halogenated hydrocarbons including solvents
No. 7	Waste from paints, pigments, glue, varnish and printing imk
No. 8	Wastes from dyes and dye-intermediates containing inorganic chemical compounds
No. 9	Wastes from dyes and dye-intermediates containing organic chemical compounds
No. 10	Waste oil and oil emulsions
No. 11	Tarry wastes from refining and tar residues from distillation or pyrolytic treatment
No. 12	Sludge arising from treatment of wastewaters containing heavy metals, toxic organics, oils emulsion and spent chemicals and incineration ash
No. 13	Phenols
No. 14	Asbestos
No. 15	Wastes from manufacturing of pesticides and herbicides and residues from pesticides and herbicides formulation units
No. 16	Acids alkalies slurry
No. 17	Off-specification and discarded products
No. 18	Discarded containers and container-liners of ha/ardous and toxic waste

Source: CPCB 1998.

Conclusion

The major industries that produce hazardous wastes include metals, chemicals, drugs and pharmaceuticals, leather, pulp and paper, electroplating, refining, pesticides, dyes, rubber goods and so on. In total, at present around 7.2 million tonnes of hazardous waste is generated in the country of which 1.4 million metric tonnes is recyclable, 0.1 million metric tonnes is incinerable and 5.2 million metric tonnes are destined for disposal on land. Improper storage, handling, transportation, treatment and disposal of hazardous waste has an adverse impact on ecosystems including the human environment. When discharged on land, heavy metals and certain organic compounds are phytotoxic and can adversely affect soil productivity for extended period of times at relatively low levels of concentration. For example, uncontrolled release of chromium contaminated wastewater and sludge resulted in contamination of aquifers in the North Arcot area in Tamil Nadu.

Projections for Solid Waste—BAU Scenario

Waste generation trends. The per capita quantity of waste generation tends to increase with time due to factors as increased commercial activities and higher standard of living. In India, the amount of waste generated per capita is estimated to increase at a rate of 1%–1.33% annually. The projected quantities of municipal solid waste for 2025 have been estimated and the scenario under the base case appears that the total waste generation in 2025 will exceed 140 million tonnes—three times the present level.

2

Environmental Pollution and Our Society

Prof. Dr. Braja Mohan Sasmal
Prof. of Chimestry
Brahmapur (Odisha)

Introduction

Before creating the living society *i.e.,* human beings, animals, birds, insects etc. on this earth, the God has created a natural surrounding or a congenial atmosphere, known as the environment, for the peaceful and healthy survival of their lives. The environment around the living society contains atmospheric air, water, soil, forests, food producing plants, trees etc. In addition to this the God has also created the biosphere, the stratosphere, ozonosphere, the vast vacuum space in which there are also sun, moon and other planets which control the climatic conditions such as light, heat, pressure, cloud formation, rainfall, oxygen content etc. which are badly needed for their existence.

Due to the rapid urbanization, huge automobile transportations, industrialization and increase of population of the living society, day by day the original purity of the constituents of the environment became impure and poisoned by inter mixing of domestic garbages and wastes, drain water, industrial wastes such as chemical effluents, smokey solids and gases, automobile exhaust gases etc. The decrease of the purity of all constituents of the environment is called as the environmental pollution. The agents that make the constuents of the environment polluted are called as pollutants.

Types of Pollution

There are two types of pollution namely:

(*a*) Conventional pollutants and

(*b*) Non-conventional pollutants.

(*a*) Conventional pollutants: The conventional or classical pollutants include domestic wastes, industrial wastes and municipal garbages which are heaped here and there without proper treatment. Untreated and partialy treated sewages from municipal wastes, water systems and safetic tanks in unsewered areas, contribute significant quantities of nutrients, suspended solid particles, dissolved solids, oils, metallic particles of heavy metals such as arsenic, mercury, lead, chromium, iron, and manganese. In addition to this nitrogen and phosphorous by over fertilization and excess use of pesticides, also come under this category.

(*b*) Non-conventional pollutants: The Non-conventional pollutants include dissolved and particulate forms of different harmful metals (both toxic and non-toxic), degradable and persistant organic carbon compounds obtained as by products of industries. Non-convetional pollutants vary from biologically inert materials such as clay and iron residues to the most toxic and insidious materials such as halogenated hydrocarbons like DDT, kepone, mirex and polychlorinated biphenyls (PCB).

By rapid growth of the population and urbanization every day the forests are being destroyed by cutting down the logs of wood and bigger trees. There by greater ecological imbalance is created causing biodiversity, global warming and frequent climatic changes in the atmosphere.

In the present days, environmental pollution is a burning problem of the world. In recent years the scientists all over the world are working seriously to control the pollution, as human beings are only responsible for creation of population. Modern techniques have been adopted to solve the pollution problems to some extent. However, public awareness will eventually force the state as well as the Central Government to implement strict acts, rules and amendments against rapid industrialization and deforestations and to adopt more effective environmental plannings and anti-pollution measures. The scientists working under Central Pollution Control Boards have already issued warnings that if the degree of environmental pollution will go on increasing at the present rate the existence of life on this earth will be questionable by the year 2020.

Classification of Pollutions

Depending on different constituents of the environment, the pollutions are classified as follows:

(*a*) Air pollution
(*b*) Water pollution
(*c*) Land pollution
(*d*) Noise or sound pollution
(*e*) Thermal pollution.

(*a*) Air pollution (Causes and Remedies): Air pollution is caused by accumulation of sufficient concentrations of poisonous gases such as carbon dioxide, carbon monoxide, nitrogen dioxide, sulphur dioxide, chlorine, bromine, methane, particles of poisonous metals and non-metals in the form of smoke in the atmospheric air. The rapid urbanization, deforestation, industrialization frequent and more use of automobiles produce these pollutants. This type of pollution is responsible for producing harmful diseases such as breathing difficulty, asthma, lungs cancer etc. and affects the paddy fields, water sources, aquatic plant and vegetations by producing acid rains during rainy days in industrial areas.

This type of pollutions can be reduced by using filters in the automobiles and industrial outlets or chimneys. Secondly the public awareness and strict government acts and rules must be implemented against deforestation and destruction of forests. Thirdly permission or license should not be issued for installation of industries near the habitats or urban areas in order to have a pollution free environment.

(*b*) Water Pollution (Causes and Remedies): Water pollution is caused by addition of dissolved or suspended solids discharging most dangerous, harmful and toxic pollutants such as detergents, pesticides, heavy metals (Mercury, Lead, Arsenic, Chromium, etc.) non-degradable, bioaccumulative compounds, domestic sewages and industrial waste chemical liquids and solids.

Excess suspended solids block out energy from the sun and effects the carbon dioxide - oxygen convention process which is vital to the maintenance of the biological food chain. Also, high concentrations of suspended solids silt up rivers, navigational channels, necessitating frequent dredging. Excess of dissolved chemical liquids and solids make the water unsuitable for cooking, drinking purpose and crop irrigation. The chemicals present in detergents, fertilizers, pesticides are harmful for food preparations and for aquatic plants and animals. The bacterias present in water will reduce the oxygen contents of water and becomes fetal for aquatic plants and animals. Water sources must be prevented from pollution carefully and sterilized by required quantities of bleaching powder and chlorine water to make it free from harmful bacterias. The domestic wastes and industrial wastes should not be mixed with the water sources and these must be sent for recycling and special treatment for purification. Moreover, the acid mixed rain water of industrial areas must not be added to the water sources during rainy season.

(*c*) Land Pollution (Causes and Remedies): Land pollution is mainly due to the earth's land surface through misuse of the soil by unsystematic agricultural practices, minings and exploitations, dumping of industrial wastes and indiscriminate disposal of urban wastes like plastics, different kinds of tinsheets, iron sheets, papers, rotten dead bodies of the animals etc. Rackless disposals of the chemical industrial wastes and wastes from paddy fields containing excess of fertilizers, insecticides and pesticides, pollute the soil of nearby area or land. Lands containing polluted soil are totally unfit for agricultural purpose. Now-a-days, the vegetables and fruits are produced are poisoned as these are produced from chemically polluted soils.

In order to check the land pollution, necessary steps must be taken not to deposit or dump the industrial and urban wastes and garbages on the open lands. These rotten wastes may be dumped in municipal dumping pits kept away from the paddy fields and urban areas.

(*d*) Noise or Sound Pollution (Causes and Remedies): The intensity of sound waves that are audible to the human ears pleasantly are called as sweet music or songs. The intensity of sound waves that are normally audible to the human ears are called as speeches. On the other hand, the sound waves of very high intensity or pitch are called as sound pollution or noise. The standard unit *i.e.,* one decibel (dB) is the intensity of sound that is just audible to the ear of an average human being.

The important causes of noise are very loudly heard sounds or blasting sounds produced by our own activities such as loud tunings of stereo systems unusual sounds of vehicle horns, sounds of supersonic jets or aeroplanes, harse announcements through loud speakers, sound of burning transformers, generators, stone and bomb blastings etc. Generally noise is produced in industrial societies more frequently, where heavy machinery, motor vehicles and aircrafts are seen functioning and moving every day. Noise pollution is more intense in working environments than in normal or peaceful environments.

Sound pollution has many psychological side effects such as hearing problem, increased irritability, lower productivity, decreased tolerance levels, increased incidence of ulcers, migraine headaches, fatigue etc.

Louder noises must be banned near the residential areas, school areas, academic institutions, offices and hospitals.

(*e*) Thermal Pollution (Causes and Remedies): When the normal temperature of the atmospheric air and the water of a particular place gets increased by radiation of heat energy form external agencies, it is called as the thermal pollution. Due to thermal pollutions the normal temperature of atmosphere air and water sources gets increased by 2 - 3 degree centigrade. The chance of thermal pollutions are more in urban and industrial areas, due to various reasons such as:

(*i*) Rapid destruction of forests and rapid urbanization which increase amount of carbon dioxide gas in the atmosphere. The heavy and thick layer of carbon dioxide gas causes green house effect in the atmosphere and does not allow the heat energy reflected from earth's surface to be released to the outer space.

(*ii*) Heavy use of motor vehicles and automobiles produce a set of exhaust gases through the outlets such as carbon monoxide, carbon dioxide, gaseous hydrocarbons etc. which check the radiations of earth's surface and heat energy to be released to the outer space by green house effect.

(*iii*) Thick and hot smokes emitted from the chimneys of the industries contain particulates of carbon, sulphur, heavy metal particles, oxides of nitrogen, sulphur dioxide and gaseous hydrocarbons which check the radiations of heat energy from earth's surface to the outer space and thereby increasing the temperature of the atmospheric air.

(*iv*) The emission of heat energy, radiations and chlorofluorocarbon gases from hugely used microwave ovens, refrigerators and airconditioners, decrease the concentrations of ozone gas from strato sphere causing number of holes in ozone layer. Through these holes the dangerous ultraviolet radiations from sun come down and reach earth's surface thereby the temperature of earth's surface is increased. This is called as global warming which very much effects the plants, animals and human beings of the earth causing sun-stroke and skin cancer.

(*v*) The hot chemical effluents coming out through the outlets of the chemical industries when disposed or added to the water sources thermal pollution occurs which kills the fishes and other aquatic animals.

Conclusion

The State as well as the central govt. should take active measures and implement strict rules to avoid such pollutions in urban and industrial areas. Further the urban and industrial wastes must be sent for special chemical treatments and re-cycling to be used for beneficial purposes of the humanity.

3

Important Role of Small Hydel Projects in Combating Effects of Climate Change

Er. Simachala Mahapatra FIE
Sapdt Engineer (Rtd.)
Managing Director
Jala Jyoti Consultancies, G2/40, Godabarisha Nagar,
Berhampur-760001

Introduction

Life survives on the planet earth due to energy from sun, which is the only source of energy in the, universe. About 30 per cent of the sun light that beams towards Earth is deflected by the outer atmosphere and scattered back to the space and the rest reaches the planet surface and is again reflected upwards, as a slow moving energy called as infrared radiation and is absorbed by the water vapour, carbondioxide, ozone and methane which ultimately slows its escape from the atmosphere. These gases are termed as "Green House Gases" and the effect of the gases in, slowing down of radiation is termed as "Green House Effect". Though the green house gases makes up only one percent of the Earth's Blanket of atmosphere, the gases regulate the climate by tapping heat and holding it like a warm water blanket. No doubt, these gases are essential environmental prerequisite of life on earth but "too much of everything is always bad". So the scientists/engineers are required to prevent or cure the unbalancing increase of these gases in the atmosphere. Actually the nature is always balanced, and all prerequisites are provided to meet the forthcoming situations. But the inhabitants, to whom these facilities are available for their use, are always misbehaving and ultimately the destruction of the natural provisions causes imbalance in nature, specifically, we the man-kind are mostly responsible, those who are only able to realize the situation. As such it is mandatory at this stage, that the human beings shall realize and rise to the occasion and work for the prevention and cure of the problem.

Before going to the topics of prevention and cure, we must consciously watch the reasons of this problem which begun when human activities distort the natural processes and also accelerate the same by adding more green house gases in the atmosphere, than that are necessary to warm the planet to an ideal temperature. This unbalancing is mainly due to following human activities to maintain the life style matching to the so called modern society:

- Burning more coal, gas and fossil fuels in transport system and in factories, causing the rise of carbondioxide level in the atmosphere.
- Change of practice, like converting agricultural lands to concrete jungle and on the other hand using more chemicals, fertilizers and pesticides to balance production. These aspects create more gases like, methane and nitrous oxide.
- Deforestation, mainly contributes to global warming, as the trees use carbondioxide and give off oxygen in its place, which helps optimal balance of gases in the atmosphere. As more forests are destroyed for timber purposes, cut down to make way for farming and the area of forest-cover drastically reduced causing imbalance of carbon-dioxide in the atmosphere.

Ultimately "Green-house gases" help in the increase of temperature in the surface of the Earth and air in the lower atmosphere. Several signs indicate that the changing of climate is all ready started. The indications are increase of water vapour in the atmosphere, glaciers and polar ice cap melting, floods and droughts becoming more severe and sea levels raised by 4 to 6" since 1990. As the statistics reveals the entire 20 century the average global temperature was increased only by 0.6

degrees Celsius and now using computer models the scientists predict that the average global temperature shall increase by 1.4 to 5.8°C at the end of AD 2100. As it stands now the percentage of the components of green house gases are as follows. Carbon dioxide is 76 per cent, Methane gas 13 per cent and the Nitrous oxide is only 6 per cent.

So in this juncture the important solution to combat the problem is to decrease the carbon dioxide emission, specifically in energy production sector.

This is only possible by producing cleaner energy through sources like Hydro-power, solar energy, wind power and waste heat utilization.

Types of Powers

Hydro-power

Currently supplying only 6 per cent of world's total source of energy, which is renewable, produced by hydraulic turbines with the force of potential energy of falling water in the natural landscapes from higher to lower elevation. It is the most clean and cheapest way of producing energy. But it also have demerits like change of flow of rivers, increase sediments and submerges forest growths. So we can take up only small hydro projects in which we can avoid all the demerits.

Wind Power

Denmark is currently the world leader in wind power. By 2030, fifty per cent of Denmark's energy could produce by wind power. Wind power emits no green house gases but it takes large amount of land and creates noise pollution and for it to make a reliable source scientists must develop better power storage techniques.

Solar Power

In the process of production of solar power, the photo voltaic cells (PVs) are being used to gather thermal energy directly from sun-rays and use the same to produce electricity. PVs don't emit green house gases but they are very expensive and more development is needed in order to bring this process to be the realistic and economic energy source in future.

Nuclear Power

This power produces no green house gases and it is a safe, clean and reliable source of energy, but it produces highly toxic radio-active wastes. More over as the raw materials for this purpose is scarce except in Europe where 42 per cent of the energy produced through fission. Overall statistics is that this power generation constitutes only 17 per cent of world electricity.

Power Generation through Waste Heat

Many industries produce heat energy by burning mainly fossil fuels. The heat so generated is utilized partly for power generation in a range of maximum up to 80 per cent. The balance 20 per cent is going as waste and to dispose the waste heat, again there are requirement of cooling towers. Now the science has been developed to use these waste heat to generate power in industries like thermal project, steel and sponge iron industries. But for its safe and economical implementation, more research and development is felt necessary.

Now from the above power sources the cleaner energy, the Hydel power appears to be more eco-friendly, economic, absolute maintenance free. Specifically, the small hydel project and mini hydel projects are very much encouraging as these projects don't destroy the landscape, minimum submergence/ no submergence. As such the small and mini hydel projects along with developing tourists spot using beautiful landscapes are the requirements of the present situation. So we discuss here some technical points, availability of finance and guide lines framed by different agencies in India, specifically in the State of Odisha where natural resources are ample.

The hydel projects are divided into four categories depending upon their generating capacity:

1. Major Hydropower Projects - Generating above 25 MW

2. Small Hydropower Projects - Generating from 1 MW to 25 MW
3. Mini Hydropower Projects - Generating 100 KW (0.1 MW) to 1 MW
4. Micro Hydropower Projects - Generating up to 100 kW

Major projects with above 25 MV capacities shall cover vast submergence of forest land and beautiful valleys attracting destruction of forests evacuation of small villages with Tribal population. It also requires heavy investment. Hence at this stage in considering present situation it is not at all feasible to take up such projects in India. In the other hand the small mini and micro projects shall be feasible to meet the requirement of rural unapproachable forest area with heavy jungle growth and natural perennial small streams.

These projects generally consist of following components:

1. A Diversion weir/barrage to regulate water for diversion for the purpose of energy generation.
2. A power channel - to carry the flow from D/W to power house site.
3. Fore bay - Approach structure to regulate the water from higher level and to utilize the available head and allowing the same in penstock.
4. Penstock - This is generally a pressure conduit connecting the fore way at higher level and the power house at lower level.
5. Power House - To accommodate all the Electro-mechanical equipments like turbine, generating equipments and valve s to control the flow.
6. Switch yard for evacuation of energy produced, to the greed substation/the area where the energy shall be used.
7. Tail race channel with stilling basin from power house to the natural nalla/valley for disposal of the water.

Conclusion

To encourage the energy production through non-conventional energies, like small Hydel projects, the ministry of non-conventional energy deptt. of Government of India allowed the private sector; joint sector and co-operative sectors to invest funds, in BOT system. The Government also allowed 20 per cent to 45 per cent of the total project cost as subsidy to them on successful completion of the projects. Government of Odisha in 2005 also framed a policy guide line for utilization of small hydel projects basing on the vision 20020 urged by the then President of India, His Excellency A.P.J. Abdul Kalam to achieve comprehensive Energy security by 2020 and total Energy Independence by 2030 using all forms of renewable energy. Basing on the guide line, many small hydel projects has been identified in the state of Orissa and entrusted to different private agencies. The IREDA and other financing Institutions are also come forward to finance the parties as soft loan and lowest possible interest. Carbon credit is also available to the enterprises.

Besides all these arrangements the progress is not that satisfactory. So it is required to create awareness among the concerned agencies and also the connected departments to go ahead towards solution of the major problem of combating the effects of the "climate change".

Global Warming and Agriculture

Prof. R.P. Sarma
Director, Institute of Economic Studies, Brahmapur-760010

Introduction

It has been estimated by the scientists that by the end of this century carbon dioxide would increase by 80 per cent of the industrial levels. The temperature would increase between 1.5 and 4.5°C during the next 25 years. The green-house gases in the atmosphere increasing rapidly since 1750 due to mainly by the three factors:

(*a*) High consumption of fossil fuels with the growth of population and advanced technology in transport system.

(*b*) New forms of different use of land, and

(*c*) Development of different types of agriculture.

The continuous increase in global warming would result in long-term changes in climate which includes the following: (1) changes in Arctic temperature and ice, (2) widespread changes in precipitation amounts, (3) salinity of the oceans, (4) wind patterns and aspects of extreme weather including draughts and heavy precipitation and (5) hot waves and intensity of tropical cyclones among others. It has been observed that Arctic temperature increasing twice as fast as global average temperature. Summer ice in arctic ocean is decreasing by 7.4 per cent per decade. By the end of this century it is predicted that in summer months the Arctic might remain ice-free in summer months. Since 1900, the seasonally frozen ground in the north Hemisphere has shrunken by about 7 per cent. Precipitation pattern has also changed during the twentieth century. There is significantly more rain in the eastern part of the North and South America, northern Europe and north and central Asia. Similarly dry spells are more frequent in the Mediterranean, South Africa and part of South Asia.

Climate Scenario

Rise of temperature globally is mainly due to the following three important factors. If there could be controlled earth's environment would be cleaner and the use of coal, gas and petroleum would be restricted the hazards of global warming can be controlled to some extent:

1. **Rapid Economic Growth:** Accelerated economic growth will bring about fast changes in the standard of living which in turn will bring about a service and information based on efficient technology. Even though international community now is very much conscious and take some policy solutions for the reduction of greenhouse gases, but then the increases in temperature may increase beyond the range of 1.1 to 2.9°C. The sea level will rise between 18 to 36 centimeters by the end of the century.
2. **Growth of Population:** People themselves are responsible for global warming. Fast growth of population put pressure on consumption of natural resources, which in turn responsible for global warming. It has been estimated the global temperature would rise 1.4 to 3.8°C. As a result sea level would increase 20 to 40 centimeters by the year 2100. But it is expected the growth of population would decline towards the second half of this century.
3. **Extensive utilization of Coal and Gas and Fossil Fuel:** Presently all activities in the society runs mostly on coal and gas in developed economies. The less developed economies fast growing and adopting these gas and coal for their daily operations. Prediction on this factor is

shocking, as it is predicted the gain of temperature due to coal and gas would be 2.4 to 6.4 degrees by the end of this century. The use of petrol and petroleum products would further increase temperature by 1.7 to 4.4°C Accordingly it is also predicted the sea level would rise 26 to 50 meters by the end of this century, which would flood the large coastal cities and islands inside the sea; while the rainfall would decrease by some 20 per cent in sub tropics.

Growth of Carbon Dioxide (CO_2)

The main instrument of global warming is increase in CO_2 in the atmosphere. Emission of CO_2 globally which was 1150 Mt. in the year 1990 increased to 1900 Mt. by the year 2005, there after the climate scientists estimated it would grow to 3300 Mt. by the year 2020; In the first 15 years it increased 750 Mt. but now it is estimated that in the next 15 years it would increase by Mt. 1400. In comparison to this increase in CO_2 in Indian atmosphere is less, in the first 15 years actual increase was 500 Mt. and in the second 15 years the estimated growth of CO_2 was 550 Mt.

Carbon dioxide emission globally and in Indian atmosphere from 1990 to 2005, actual and estimated emission from 2005 to 2020 by climate scientists is presented in Table 4.1.

Table 4.1: Global and India's CO_2 Emissions : 1990-2020

Sl. No.	Year	Mt. CO_2 Global	Growth Per cent	Mt. CO_2 India	Growth Per cent
1	1990	1150	—	1200	—
2	1995	1300	33.80	1300	8.33
3	2000	1550	19.23	1500	15.38
4	2005	1900	22.58	1700	13.33
5	2010	2300	26.31	1800	5.88
6	2015	2800	34.78	2250	25.00
7	2020	3300	17.85	2550	13.33

Source: International Report on Climate Change (IPCC, 2000-2010, New York.

Even if the growth of carbon dioxide is lower in India, but it cannot be eliminate the hazards of climate change in the country. Some of the hazards of climate change to be faced are:

- A one meter rise in sea level water can displace lakhs people along the sea coast.
- The Gangotry glacier, the source of river Ganga is retreating at a speed of about 30 meters per year now, with warming temperature likely to increase the rate of melting further.
- Annual coal consumption in India is rapidly increasing and has more than tripled since 1980 and further increase its utilization may create problems.
- India's carbon dioxide emission have increased by 78 per cent since 1990. Of course per capita emission in India is only 2 tonnes in comparison to 25 tonnes and 11 tonnes in U.S.A. and U.K. respectively. But unless India now checks the emission on a war footing, by the year 2025 India would be one of the top three green-house-emitting countries in the world.

Climate Change and Agriculture

Emission of green-house-gas warms the atmosphere which affects the plants and agriculture and in turn affects human beings. Some deadliest affects of global warming have already being started and unless preventive measures are taken it would destroy forests and also human beings in the long run. Few of the affects can be mentioned here:

1. **Spread of diseases:** the warmth of atmosphere the disease carrying insects start migrating north with plague and other germs carrying with them. Malaria cannot be fully eradicated because of continuously increasing global warm.
2. **Warmer waters and more hurricanes**, because of rise of temperature of the oceans.

3. **Increased probability of droughts and heat waves.** Africa will receive the worst of it and more sever droughts are also expected in Europe.
4. **Polar ice caps melting** would bring greater damages to earth. The dangers are: (1) it will raise sea level. (2) Ice caps would be melted and desalinize the ocean. (3) Rise in temperature changes landscape in arctic circle which will endanger several species of animals. (4) The ice-caps reflect sun-light, much of it relent back into space which would further cool down the earth. With the ice-caps are gone it would further warm the atmosphere.

The nature of atmosphere in the world in the year 2050 and how it affect agriculture which is the basis for food of the human beings are analyzed by the climate and earth scientists are summarized in Table 4.2.

Table 4.2 : Effects of Global Warming on Agriculture

Sl. No.	Climatic Element	Expected change By 2050	Effect on Agriculture
1.	Carbon Dioxide	Increase from 360 ppm to 450-600 ppm	1. Increased Photosynthesis 2. Reduced water use
2.	Sea level rise	Rise by 10-12 CM	1. Loss of land 2. Coastal erosion 3. Floods 4. Saline of ground water
3.	Temperature	Rise by 1 – 2°C Increase frequency of Heat waves	1. Faster, shorter, earlier 2. Growing season 3. Heat stress risk 4. Increased evapo-transpiration
4.	Precipitation	Seasonal changes by ± 10%	1. Impact on droughts 2. Risk soil workability 3. Water logging
5.	Storminess	Increased wind speed specially in the north and more intense rainfall	1. Lodging 2. Soil erosion 3. Reduced infiltration of Rainfall

Source: IPCC Reports, 2000-2009, New York.

Increase in carbon dioxide in the atmosphere, rise in sea level and increases in temperature that would bring about ten specific changes on the living beings on earth specified in Table 4.2 clearly indicates how the agriculture would be affected by the year 2050 unless precautions are taken promptly by the nations. In simple terms global warming effect agricultural through, (1) changes in soil water system, (2) water deficits would directly effect fruit and vegetable production and (3) livestock population specially poultry and pigs would be exposed to higher incidence of heat stress influencing productivity.

The Dilemma for India

Accelerated economic, growth certainly alleviates poverty in India which is the most important problem now. The economic planners cannot think of slowing down the development process to control green-house gases. Present trend of economic growth in India is expected energy consumption of four times higher by 2030 at the present 2005 levels. With this backdrop India is resisting international pressure to curb its green-house emissions. As a developing economy India is exempted from mandatory caps on emission. In per capita emission of green-house gas Indian emissions are less than 10 per cent of American economies. India is now stressing the developed economies to take action to reduce their emissions first so that India and other developing countries would follow. Most of the developing economies are now in dilemma whether to have accelerated economic growth or environmental protection. If environment is not protected the long-term economic growth will be hampered, on the other hand when economic growth is given priority the degradation of environment would create sufferings for the people. India is not badly affected by the economic crisis as Indian planners adopted different strategy of economic growth path in which the economy is heavily dependent on agriculture and not too much export oriented. If India can invent a new model of economic growth path, a model where one need not first destroy the environment and then invest in cleaning it up with accelerated economic growth it would be boon to the world. If at all possible, it is far away a dream.

REFERENCES

1. Walther *et al.*, Ecological Responses to Recent Climate Change, *Nature*, 416, March, 2002.
2. Drew Harrell *et al.*, Climate Warming and Diseases Risk for Trrestrial and Marine Biota, *Science* 296, Jan. 2002.
3. IPCC, *International Panel on Climate Change Report*, 2000, 2007, 2009, New York.
4. GLORIA, Global Observation Research Initiative in Alpine Environment, *Research Observation, 2008*.

5

Forests and Environment
A Study

Dr. Prafulla Chandra Mohanty
Principal (Rtd.), Ganjam College, Ganjam, Odisha

Introduction

Forests are the important resources of a country. It is counted as the one of the valuable assets of the nation. Forest creates environment and environment creates climate. So both are inter-dependent. Forest boosts the economy in many respects. It directly effects the environment, the climate and observes lot of wastes and allows the living species in good and comfortable health. Forests produce a lot of products which add to our economical status. It habitates wildlife, medicinal plants etc. In some countries, forests became the backbone of their economies. "Forests are close formation of trees growing together at one place". It is very important for the national economy of any country of the world. Like the farms it provides raw-materials to some specific industries dealing with the manufacturing of rubber, paper, artificial textiles, medicines, etc. It is marked that the economy of some countries like Norway, Sweden, Canada, Finland, U.S.S.R. etc. largely depend on their forest resources. So, forestry has started to develop as a special branch in almost all the countries of the world and the countries having deficiency in forests are trying to develop it artificially. A total of 7485 million acres of land are covered by forests in the world. Out of this 2090 million acres are in Asia, 774 millions acres are in Europe, 797 million acres are in Africa, 2092 million acres are in South America, 1449 million acres are in North America and 283 million acres are in Australia. Thus 28 per cent of the total forest area of the world is in Asia. Ten per cent is in Europe, 11 per cent is in Africa, 28 per cent is in South America, 19 per cent is in North America only a 4 per cent is in Australia.

India has a vast forest area. Out of its total area of 32.80 lakh square kilometres, 7.53 lakh sq. of land is covered by forests. Thus the total forest area is about 23 per cent. Now it is reduced to 22.1 per cent by A.D. 2000) of the country. This forest area is classified as of 83 per cent accessible and 17 per cent as of inaccessible. The forests of Assam, Karnataka, Odisha, West Bengal, Bihar, Jharkhand, Chhattisgarh, U.P., Madhya Pradesh and Andhra Pradesh etc. are of accessible nature and of Himachal Pradesh, North East India and Jammu and Kashmir have been still remaining in inaccessible for the human beings. On the basis of ownership, 96 per cent of the total forest area belongs to State Governments and the rest 4 per cent belongs to corporate bodies and private individuals.

Importance of Forests

Forest is not merely an ancillary activity to agriculture. Forests occupy an important position in the economy of a country. In India, where forestry is a less important primary activity, its contribution to net national product is around 1.0 per cent. It provides direct employment to more than 1 lakh persons and another 3 lakh persons are of in partly employment. Forest is the source of fodder for about 3 crore cattle. Industrial and fuel wood is the main forest product. Fuel wood still remains the main source of energy for consumption in rural areas. Apart from providing industrial wood for wood based industries, forests are also a source of a number of minor products like bamboo. canes, grasses, kendu leaves, lac, resins, medicinal plants, qums, ganning materials, dyes, essential oils, fatty oils and fat etc. The demand for some of these minor forest products exists in foreign markets and if their output is stepped up, they can prove to be valuable foreign exchange earners. Forests also confer a variety of ecological benefits. They moderate the climate of the region and reduce the extremes of the temperature. Presence of forest in a region increases humidity in air, and reduces the uncertainity element in rainfall. Trees suck a lot of water during rains which raises the underground water level. Forests also prevent soil erosion because they check flow of water. Forests reduce the intensity of floods, as they regulate the supply of water in streams and reservoirs. Again water flowing through forests carries with it highly fertile soil, which is left behind in agricultural fields raises their fertility. In substance, forests have an immense environmental value. Their indiscriminate destruction in any country can disturb the ecological balance and play havoc with the economic life of the country. In this context a paper is made to study the importance of forests and the sizes of forests in the nation as well as in the State of Odisha, its different uses and abuses (deforestation). The paper also tries to highlight on the State-wise distribution of forests in India, geographical distributions, different feorest products, it's effect on bio-diversity and on some of the deforestation statistics. Towards the end it narrates different problems issues and comments with a conclusion.

Forests have a many-faced ecological role to play which affects human life directly. They create the dangers of cloud drifting, soil erosion, floods, wind erosion and groundwater evaporation. They also protect a wide variety of flora and fauna, provide recreation and can effectively control air pollution of moderate magnitude. Thus importance of forests for the benefit of mankind as well as for other forms of life cannot be over emphasized.

India's population has risen from 370 million in 1947 to 1100 million in 2006, constituting more than 18 per cent of the world population. India also has 15 per cent of world's livestock, but only 2 per cent of the geographical area, one per cent of forest area, and 0.5 per cent of pasture lands. Per capita availability of forest in India is 0.07 hactres by the year A.D. 2000 as per government of India survey, which is much lower than the world average of

0.8 ha India has a forest area of 64 million ha. which constitutes only 19.5 per cent of the total land area at present as against 33 per cent of National Forest Policy of 1988. Closed type of forest having forest cover density of 40 per cent or more is approximately only 11 per cent of the country's total land area. The average annual production of wood per hactre is 0.7 m^3 (cubic metre) as compared to the world average of 2.1 m^3. It has been estimated that about 157 million tonnes of firewood are required for fuel every year by the rural population, whereas production is only 58 million tonnes. (Government of India 1993). The remaining demand is met by illegal cutting and encroachment of the forest. Though there are some trends in the area of an improvement in the quality of forest, there is still need to have massive reforestation programmes, control over hacking and gracing and provision of cheap fuel through alternative techologies such as Solar Power or bio-gas plants, more kerosene and LPG should be made available to save the forest from deforestation.

Soil is the non-renewable natural resource which supports practically all terrestrial plant life and consequently human life. About 130 million ha. of land (45% of the geographical area) is affected by serious soil erosion through ravine and gully, shifting, cultivation, cultivated waste lands, sandy areas, deserts and water logging. This results in soil degradation. Under favourable conditions in India, it takes almost a thousand years to form only 2.3 cm of soil layer from wheathered rocks. It is reported that the loss of one mm of cultivated soil could cost 10 kg of nitrogen and 2 kg of phosphorous.

India has a rich heritage of species and genetic strains of flora and fauna. Overall 8 per cent of world species are found in India. It is estimated that India is tenth among the plant rich countries of the world, eleventh in terms of number of endemic species of higher vertebrates and sixth among the centres of diversity and origin of agribiodiversity. The total number of living species identified in India so far as 2,00,000. Out of the total twelve bio-diversity hot spots in the world, India has two, one in the north east region and other is the Western Ghat region. But as the forests are becoming bare, many of these are fast becoming extinct or coming to the verge of extinction. These species and varieties provide a challenge to geneticists, animal behaviourists, botanists, zoologists, economists and many others who have a lot to learn about and from them. About 1143 animals comprising 71 species of mamals, 88 species of birds and five species of reptiles as rare and endangered wild animals. Similarly, many plant species, which have forests as their sustaining source, are also disappearing rapidly. To preserve them, special bio-reserves should be created.

India's environment is drastically attacked and destroyed during the past 60 years of time by the process of deforestation. According to FAO, India was supposed to have lost 3.4 million ha of forest land between 1950 to 1972 alone. During the period over 7 per cent of forest area was lest due to agriculture and other 17 per cent was past due to river valley projects, industries, roads and communications. Till to-day the process of deforestation has continued at the current annual rate of 1.3 to 1.5 million ha A recent report of international union for the conservation of nature and natural resources (IUCN) mentions that India has lost 2.5 million ha of mangrove forests in this century alone. It has been estimated that inorder to maintain the balance at least 10 million ha of degraded land need to be brought under forest per annum.

Forest in Odisha

The forest ecosystem in Odisha is depleting at a much faster rate than it being remedied by taking of plantation. The impact of various sectors of denudation have brought in a change in the traditional system of management of the forests as well as other natural resources like land, water, etc. This is happening at a time when the whole social fabric is under severe strain because of ignorance, poverty, unemployment, underemployment and unproductive employment, particularly of the rural poor in and around forest areas. The recorded forest area of Odisha has undergone following changes :

1970-71	72,800 sq. km
1977-78	67,675 sq. km
1980-81	59,693 sq. Km
1984-85	59,555 sq. km
1988-89	57,183.57 sq. km
1995-96	56,059 52 sq. km
2005-06	50,000 sq. km (Projectd)

Source: Reference Odisha, p. 16

Forest Problems

The biggest problem of the Indian forests is the inadequate and fast dwindling forest cover. It has already been mentioned that forests cover only 23.43 per cent of the area against the required coverage of 33 per cent. Even this small percentage of forest cover is seriously threatended by the increasing demand for major and minor forest products. These products are badly needed for fuel, building and to feed a large number of forest based industries. Vast forest tracts have been cleared for agriculture. Shifting agriculture in different parts of the country has played havoc with forests. Overgrazing is a big factor which is responsible for serious damage to forests. India possesses a livestock population of over 412 million of which 270 million are bovine animals, about one-tenth of which graze in the forests. Whenever forests are easily accessible, the livestock entirely depends on grazing in them.

The forests are thick, inaccessible, slow growing and lack in gregarious stands in many parts of the country. Some of them are very thin and comprise only of thorny bushes. These factors make their utilization uneconomical because there is good deal of wastage and it makes very expensive in spite of the cheap labour available in India.

One of the biggest problems faced by the Indian forests is the lack of proper transport facilities. About 16 per cent of the forest land in India is inaccessible and does not have proper transport facilities. It must be remembered that the major product of the forests is timber which is a cheap and bulky commodity. As such it cannot afford high freight charges by the railways and roadways. Therefore, they cannot be economically exploited without the availability of cheap and efficient transport facilities. Unfortunately, in India. The railways serve thickly populated areas only and are not of much use to forests. All weather roads in the forest areas are badly lacking. Water transport has only limited scope. Considering these facts we can easily say that transport with reference to forests is inadequate in India. Large tracts of vegetal cover are destroyed every year by forest fires. Forest fires in India are most destructive in dry season. Insufficiency of properly trained personnel is also a big handicap.

Conclusion

Forests give life to living beings. In order to carry on a living society in the living world, it is required to stay with plants. if this rate of dangerous deforestation. Global warming etc. will continue the living society will in no time collapse. So it is highly essential in the present days to protect forests.

Table 5.1 : Estimates of Wastelands in India (Lakh Hectare)*
Statewise Forests and Non-Forest Degraded Areas

States	Non-Forest Degraded Area	Rank (Top Ten)	Forest Degraded Area	Rank (Ton Ten)	Total	Bank
Andhra Pradesh	76.8	5	37.3	2		4
Assam	9.3	—	7.9	—	17.3	—
Bihar	39.0	8	15.6	8	54.6	8
Gujarat	78.4	4	6.8	—	78.4	6
Haryana	24.0	—	0.7	—	24.8	—
Himachal Pradesh	14.2	—	5.3	—	19.6	—
Jammu & Kashmir	5.3	—	10.3	—	15.7	—
Karnataka	71.2	6	20.4	6	91.6	—
Kerala	10.5	—	2.3	—	12.8	—
Madhya Pradesh	129.5	2	72.0	1		1
Maharashtra	115.6	3	28.4	4		3

...(*Contd.*)

Manipur	0.1	—	14.2	10	14.4	—
Meghalaya	8.1	—	11.0	—	19.2	—
Nagaland	5.1	—	8.8	—	13.9	—
Odisha	31.6	10	32.3	3	63.9	7
Punjab	11.5	—	0.8	—	12.3	—
Rajasthan	180.0	1	19.3	7		2
Sikkim	1.3	—	1.5	—	2.8	—
Tamil Nadu	34.0	9	10.1	—	44.0	9
Tripura	1.1	—	8.6	—	9.7	—
Uttar Pradesh	66.3	7	14.3	9	80.6	5
West Bengal	22.0	—	3.6	—	25.4	—
Union Territory	8.9	—	27.1	5	36.0	10
Total	**937.0**		**358.9**			

*Includes wasteland due to natural causes and desert areas of Rajasthan.
Source: Government of India (1989), *Developing India's Wastelands*, Ministry of Environment and Forests, New Delhi.

REFERENCES

1. *District at a Glance*, 2005, Orissa, Government of Orissa Directorate of Economics and Statistics.
2. *Environmental Studies*, B.P. Satapathy & Amiya Prasad Das.
3. *Fundamentals of Environmental Studies* by S.N. Tripathy and Surnakar Panda, 2005, Vrinda Publications Pvt. Ltd.
4. *Indian Development Report*, 1997, K. Parikh Indira Gandhi Institute of Developmenr Research.
5. *Indian Economy* : Rudra Dutta, 2006 Ed. & KPM Sundaram.
6. *Indian Economy* : S.K. Mishra & V.K. Puri, 2003 Edn., p. 103, Himalaya Publishing House, Bombay.
7. *'Reference Orissa"* : An Indian State of Eastern Region published by Enterprising Publishers.
8. *Statesman*, of 21.03.06, p. 6.
9. *The Pearson General Knowledge Manual*, 2004.
10. *World Resources* by M.S. Kar, Books & Books, Cuttack.

6

A Study of Industrial Water Pollution in India

G. Chandrayya
Selection Grade Lecturer in Commerce
Government College (A), Rajahmundry, A.P.

Introduction

During the past few decades Indian industries have registered a quantum jump, which has contributed to high economic growth but simultaneously it has also given rise to severe environmental pollution. Consequently, ambient air and water quality is seriously affected which is far lower in comparison to the international standards. The problem is worse in the case of water pollution. It is found that one-third of the total water pollution comes in the form of effluent discharge, solid wastes and other hazardous wastes. Untreated or allegedly treated effluents have increase the level of toxins in like cyanide and chromium up to 20 times the safe level in 22 critically polluted areas of the country. The surface water is the main source of industries for waste disposal. It is found that almost all rivers are polluted in most of the stretches by some industry or the other. Although all industries function under the strict guidelines of the Central Pollution Control Board (CPCB) but still the environmental situation is far from satisfactory. Different norms and guidelines are given for all the industries depending upon their pollution potentials. In India there are sufficient evidences available related with the mismanagement of industrial wastes. Consequently, at the end of each time period the pollution problem takes menacing concern. The conventional methods so far adopted for the assessment of environmental quality (air, water) have considered only the aspect of direct pollution output. The sectors with high discharge of direct pollution are given uniform treatment under the category of highly polluting sectors. The difference that arises because of indirect effect during the process of production has been completely ignored. Moreover, most of the studies undertaken in the Indian context have been very broad and aggregative in nature. There have been very few attempts to study the industrial pollution at a disaggregated level. So far no clear-cut estimations have been made to determine the overall effects of the industrial pollution, especially industrial water pollution. In very few instances the problem has been identified partially.

Direct pollution effect implies generation of pollution per unit of output in a particular sector. Indirect effects are generated not in an industry in which production takes place directly but in those industries whose output is used as an input in the production process of a particular industry. These effects are important to consider because the overall quality of the environment greatly depends upon the total effect (direct plus indirect). This dissertation presents an analysis of industrial water pollution by way of input-output technique for the period 1983-84 to 1993-94.

Objectives of the Study

The main objectives of the study are:

(1) to study the water pollution intensity and thereby to study the nature of inter-relationships among the different sectors of the input-output table of the Indian economy;

(2) to examine the nature of technical change and its consequence on pollution generation over a period of time; and

(3) to examine the status of pollution control through different abatement techniques.

The term pollution intensity has been used to indicate the total (direct plus indirect) generation of pollution. The pollution intensity intends to explain units of the physical pollution output expressed in money value of economic sectors. Thus, these units indicate generation of pollution in cu.m. tonnes per lakh rupees of output.

For the above-mentioned objectives open, static Leontief type input-output model is applied. Input-output (I-O) model is essentially a simplified model of production, which takes into account the interdependencies among producing sectors of the economy. The output of a particular sector depends upon two things - firstly, the amount of quantity demanded by the consumers or households and secondly, the input requirements of the other sectors of the economy using the output of that sector as an input. Generation of pollution is a regular feature of the production and consumption process and thus, can be referred as an undesirable by product of the activities. The level of pollution directly varies with the level of output. Any change in the output level of pollutants is the results of either a change in the final demand of specific goods and services or changes in the technological structure of one or more sectors of the economy, or a change in the combination of these two factors. For the present purpose I-O model of the generalized nature has been considered, where sxtra rows and columns are used to represent the generation and abatement of pollution. The models of the Leontief (1970) and Leontief and Ford (1972) are of this kind. The technological effects have been studied by using the Carter (1970) and Forssell (1988) I-O's approach.

Industrial Pollution

Empirically, very little use has been made of I-O technique to study the industrial pollution. In most of the empirical literature energy-based emissions have studied. Gay and Proops (1993), Proops (1996), Wier (1998), Ostblom (1998), have concentrated their work on the factors associated with energy emissions. There have very few attempts to study the cumulative pollution intensities. Though the studies of Leontief and Ford (1972) for the USA, Miernyk and Sears (1974) for West Virginia USA; James *et al.*, (1978) for Netherlands; Forsund and Strom (1974) for Norway, have made such attempts. But most of these studies have been conducted for the air pollutants. No such attempts have been made on water pollutants. In India too there are very few descriptions and studies available for industrial water pollutants. Murthy *et. al.,* (1997a, 1997b) have made some attempts and applied I-O techniques for the analysis of the consequences of economic development on carbon-dioxide emissions.

The data utilized in the present study is provided by the Central Statistical Organization (CSO) in the form of Input-Output Transaction Table (IOTT) for the years 1983-84, 1989-90 and 1993-94. These tables can best be described as open, static Leontief type tables. The commodity-by-commodity input-output tables have been used for the present purpose. In order to make all tables consistent with each other for comparison, these tables have been converted to the common base at 1993-94 prices. Center for Monitoring Indian Economy (CME 1989, 1991, 1994) price indices and National Accounts Statistics (NAS) figures have been used for this purpose. Another adjustment is done in terms of number of sectors; original 115 sectors of the IOTT have been condensed to 56. These sectors are formed on the basis of their environmental consequences and also on economic rationale. The final demand category has five components-private final consumption expenditure (PFCE), government final consumption expenditure (GFCE), gross investments (GI), exports (EXP) and imports (IMP).

The other data used in the study for the creation of environment matrix have been collected from various secondary sources. However, the main sources have been Central Pollution Board (CPCB) and Uttar Pradesh State Pollution Control Board (SPCB). The environment matrix has been formed for 36 different organic, inorganic and toxic water pollutants. Thus, the analysis has been performed for 56 sectors with 36 water pollution parameters. There are three categories of industries found, viz. non-polluting, highly polluting and low/moderately polluting. Out of 56 sectors 6 sectors appear to be non-polluting.

26 sectors are highly polluting and remaining sectors are low/ moderately polluting.

In the first instance we have analyzed the direct pollution intensity. The analysis shows that most of the direct pollution is generated by the sectors of the highly polluting category. Other moderately or low-polluting sectors are responsible for only small proportion of pollution generation. Sectors such as, dairy, beverages, textile, paper, leather, rubber, heavy chemicals, fertilizers, drugs, synthetic fiber etc., are responsible for most of the pollution in the economy.

The analysis on total (direct plus indirect) water pollution intensity has been performed from two perspectives - firstly, the interaction effect of all the sectors has been calculated by taking the direct pollution coefficients of all the sectors at a time and secondly, separate analysis has also been performed for highly polluting sectors. This has been done by taking the pollution coefficients of highly polluting sectors by and assuming pollution from other (low/moderately-polluting sectors) sectors to be zero.

The results regarding total (direct plus indirect) water pollution intensity have also confirmed the previous results obtained in the case of direct pollution intensity. Again highly polluting sectors appear to be major polluting sectors. Three important categories of sectors have clearly emerged from this analysis. Firstly, sectors in which there is high direct and high indirect effect. Secondly, sectors in which there is high direct effect but indirect effect is not very significant. Thirdly, there are sectors in which direct pollution intensity is very low but the indirect intensity component is very high. All these categories are cause of concern. The uniqueness of the input-output technique is in finding the third category.

The total water pollution intensity results of highly polluting sectors indicate that not much difference is observed after eliminating the direct polluting effect of low/moderately polluting sectors. This shows that most of the pollution in the economy is generated by the inter-relatedness of the highly polluting sectors. If pollution of highly polluting sectors can be possibly controlled then the overall situation of the rising industrial effluents can also be controlled to an extent.

The final demand intensity has also been analyzed in order to find the contribution of each component of final demand category in total pollution generation. If we divide the entire final demand category into three parts viz., consumption (private plus government), investments and exports then we find that major portion is held by the consumption category in which private final consumption expenditure (PFCE) appear to be most dominant.

The next objective is to study the effect of technological change on pollution generation. The production function approach of the input-output technique has been followed for the assessment of technological change on pollution generation. The analysis has been done by taking the structural coefficient matrices at two different time periods and final demand vector is kept constant at the base period. The level of pollution is then compared from two different structural coefficient matrices. This analysis has been performed at aggregated as well as at disaggregated level for 36 water pollution parameters of the 56 sectors of the I-O table. For the purpose of analysis the entire period has been divided into two sub-period viz. 1983-84 to 1989-90 and 1989-90 to 1993-94. Separate analysis covering entire period from 1983-84 to 1993-94 has also been done.

It is fond that over a period of time the input technology has not been environment friendly. Even in highly polluting sectors the pollution growth has been very high. The technology deterioration in terms of environmental pollution is more prominent during the first sub-period. During second sub-period some improvement has been observed. The analysis covering entire period again indicates deterioration in technology over a period of time. During 1983-84 to 1989-90 agriculture, other services, construction, dairy, sugar, edible oil, food products, beverages, tobacco, textile, jute, leather, rubber, plastic, fertilizers, paints and varnishes, drugs and medicines, other chemical, synthetic fibre and batteries have been shown highest growth in pollution output as a result of technological change.

During the second sub-period many industries under the highly polluting industrial category have given sign of improvement with 1993-94 technology in comparison to 1989-90 technology. The industries that have been present with high positive growth of pollution have now started showing negative trend for the majority of the pollutants. Industries such as sugar, food products, beverages, plastic, fertilizer, drugs and medicine, are important among them. The most drastic change is being observed in case of other services and construction.

The results covering entire period from 1983-84 to 1993-94 are very much similar to the results of the first sub-period *i.e.,* 1983-84 to 1989-90, Again pollution growth in most of the highly polluting sectors has been on rise. No gains of technological change have been observed on the pattern of pollution generation.

The next objective is to analyze the pollution control status in the economy. For this purpose data on three abatement techniques has been collected. The first two techniques show secondary level pollution abatement and third technique reflects the level of abatement when tertiary level treatment is undertaken. The actual data on three abatement techniques could be obtained only for 12 sectors and 5 water pollution parameters. With this level of pollution is calculated from three alternative abatement techniques and their efficiency of pollution abatement is calculated. Two exercises have been performed-firstly, the difference in pollution abatement from three different abatement techniques is calculated and their efficiency is compared in terms of pollution abatement. Secondly, the status of pollution abatement is being examined by comparing the actual pollution intensity with the pollution intensity of the three abatement techniques.

The results shows that third abatement technique is at least 8-10 per cent more efficient in the case of biological and chemical oxygen demand (BOD and COD), in comparison to first and second technique. This implies that if it is possible to employ the tertiary level effluent treatment in some of the sectors then pollution can be reduced to a great extent. The actual pollution intensity is several times greater than the pollution intensity of three abatement techniques. The overall situation of pollution abatement in the economy is not very satisfactory.

Conclusion

The findings of the present study can be useful for the formulation of environment policy and design of the production system. This gives an idea to the policy makers about the water pollution consequences of the past and provides a basis for the future policy at aggregated as well as disaggregated level.

7

Health Effects of Air Pollution

P. Divakara Rao
Lecturer in Commerce, Government Degree College, Tuni, East Godavarin District, Andhra Pradesh

M. Srinuvasu
Lecturer in Commerce Degree College, Tuni, East Godavari District, Andhra Pradesh

Introduction

The human health effects of poor air quality are far reaching, but principally affect the body's respiratory system and the cardiovascular system. Individual reactions to air pollutants depend on the type of pollutant a person is exposed to the degree of exposure, the individual's health status and genetics. People who exercise outdoors, for example, on hot, smoggy days increase their exposure to pollutants in the air.

The health effects caused by air pollutants may range from subtle biochemical and physiological changes to difficulty breathing, wheezing, coughing and aggravation of existing respiratory and cardiac conditions. These effects can resul in increased medication use, increased doctor or emergency room visits, more hospital admissions and even premature death.

- Human Respiratory System
- Human Cardiovascular System

- Heart and Lung Diseases
- Pyramid of Health Effects
- Populations at Risk
- Leading Causes of Hospitalization
- Leading Causes of Death
- Estimating Health Benefits.

Human Respiratory System

The health of our lungs and entire respiratory system is affected by the quality of the air we breathe. In addition to oxygen, this air contains other substances such as pollutants, which can be harmful. Exposure to chemicals by inhalation can negatively affect our lungs and other organs in the body. The respiratory system is particularly sensitive to air pollutants because much of it is made up of exposed membrane. Lungs are anatomically structured to bring large quantities of air (on average, 400 million litres in a lifetime) into intimate contact with the blood system, to facilitate the delivery of oxygen.

Lung tissue cells can be injured directly by air pollutants such as ozone, metals and free radicals. Ozone can damage the alveoli—the individual air sacs in the lung where oxygen and carbon dioxide are exchanged. More specifically, airway tissues which are rich in bioactivation enzymes can transform organic pollutants into reactive metabolites and cause secondary lung injury. Lung tissue has an abundant blood supply that can carry toxic substances and their metabolites to distant organs. In response to toxic insult, lung cells also release a variety of potent chemical mediators that may critically affect the function of other organs such as those of the cardiovascular system. This response may also cause lung inflammation and impair lung function.

Structure and Function

The human respiratory system is dominated by our lungs, which bring fresh oxygen (CO_2) into our bodies while expelling carbon dioxide (CC_2). The oxygen travels from the lungs through the bloodstream to the cells in all parts of the body. The cells use the oxygen as fuel and give off carbon dioxide as a waste gas. The waste gas is carried by the bloodstream back to the lungs to be exhaled.

The lungs accomplish this vital process—called gas exchange—using an automatic and quickly adjusting control system. This gas exchange process occurs in conjunction with the central nervous system (CNS), the circulatory system and the musculature of the diaphragm and the chest.

The human respiratory system can be divided into the upper respiratory tract and the lower respiratory tract. The upper respiratory tract includes the following rigid structures:

Nasal cavities: Filter the air we breathe and provide a sense of smell.

Pharynx: Acts in the respiratory and the digestive system.

Larynx: Link between the pharynx and the trachea. Generates the voice with the presence of vocal folds.

Trachea: The trachea is the bond with the lower respiratory tract. This is a flexible structure allowing the air to go down to the lungs.

In addition to gas exchange, the lungs and the other parts of the respiratory system have important jobs to do related to breathing. These include:

- Bringing all air to the proper body temperature.
- Moisturizing the inhaled air for necessary humidity.
- Protecting the body from harmful substances by coughing, sneezing, filtering or swallowing them, or by alerting the body through the sense of smell.
- Defending the lungs with cilia (tiny hair-like structure), mucus and macrophages, which act to remove harmful substances deposited in the respiratory system.

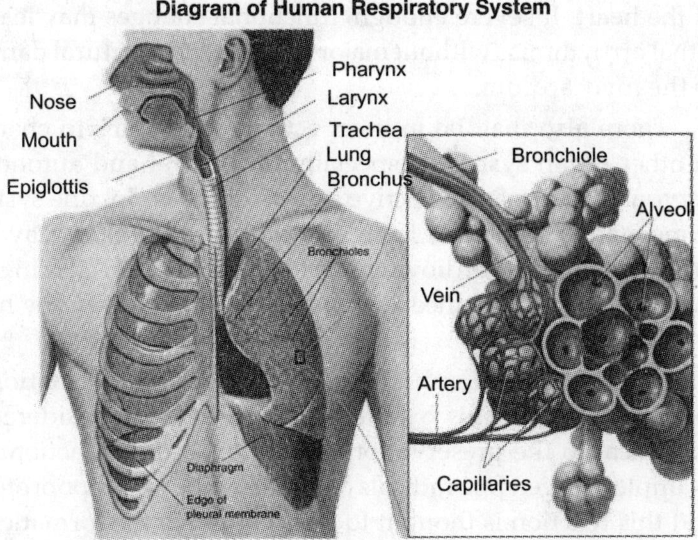

The respiratory system is sensitive to air pollution. The cardiovascular system can be affected as well.

Human Cardiovascular System

The cardiovascular system has two major components: the heart and a network of blood vessels. The cardiovascular system supplies the tissues and cells of the body with nutrients, respiratory gases, hormones and metabolites and removes the waste products of cellular metabolism as well as foreign matter. It is also responsible for maintaining the optimal internal homeostasis of the body and the critical regulation of body temperature and pH.

The inhalation of air pollutants eventually leads to their absorption into the bloodstream and transport to the heart. A wide spectrum of chemical and biological substances may interact directly with the cardiovascular system to cause structural changes, such as degenerative necrosis and inflammatory reactions. Some pollutants may also directly cause functional alterations that affect the rhythmicity and contractility of the heart. If severe enough, functional changes may lead to lethal arrhythmias without major evidence of structural damage to the myocardium.

There also may be indirect actions secondary to changes in other organ systems, especially the central and autonomic nervous systems and selective actions of the endocrine system. Some cytokins released from other inflamed organs may also produce adverse cardiovascular effects, such as reducing the mechanical performance and metabolic efficiency of the heart and blood vessels.

Many chemical substances may cause the formation of reactive oxygen. This oxidative metabolism is considered to be critical to the preservation of cardiovascular function. For example, oxygen free radicals oxidize low-density lipoproteins, and this reaction is thought to be involved in the formation of the atherosclerotic plaques. Oxidized low-density lipoproteins can injure blood vessel cells and increase adherence and the migration of inflammatory cells to the injured area. The production of oxygen free radicals in heart tissues have been associated with arrhythmias and heart cell death.

Heart and Lung Diseases

Heart and lung illnesses and diseases are common in Canada, and there are many factors that can increase the chances of contracting them such as smoking and genetic predisposition. The role of air pollution as the underlying cause remains unclear but is the subject of considerable research. However, it is clear that air pollution, infections and allergies can exacerbate these conditions. An early diagnosis can lead to appropriate treatment and ensure a normal or close to normal quality of iife. In many cases however, there is no cure and those affected may die prematurely. The following are the most prevalent diseases:

Minor Lung Illnesses - the common cold is the most familiar of these, with symptoms including sore throat, stuffy or runny nose, coughing and sometimes irritation of the eyes.

Lung Infections - croup, bronchitis, and pneumonia are caused by viruses or bacteria and are very common. Symptoms may include cough, fever, chills and shortness of breath.

Asthma - is an increasingly common chronic disease among children and adults. It causes shortness of breath, coughing or wheezing or whistling in the chest. Asthma attacks can be triggered by a variety of factors including exercise, infection, pollen, allergies and stress. It can also be triggered by a sensitivity to non-allergic types of pollutants present in the air such as smog.

Chronic Obstructive Pulmonary Disease (COPD) - is also known as chronic obstructive lung disease and encompasses two major disorders: emphysema and chronic bronchitis. Emphysema is a chronic disorder in which the walls and elasticity of the alveoli are damaged. Chronic bronchitis is characterized by inflammation of the cells lining the inside of bronchi, which increases the risk of infection and obstructs airflow in and out of the lung. Smoking is responsible for approximately 80 per cent of COPD cases while other forms of air pollution may also influence the development of these diseases. Symptoms include cough, production of mucous and shortness of breath. It is important to note that no cure exists for people suffering from COPD although healthy lifestyle and appropriate medication can help.

Lung Cancer - is the most common cause of death due to cancer in women and men. Cigarette smoke contains various carcinogens and is responsible for most cases of this often fatal disease. The symptoms of lung cancer begin silently and then progress to chronic cough, wheezing and chest pain. Air pollution has been linked somewhat weakly to lung cancer.

Coronary Artery Disease - refers to the narrowing or blocking of the arteries or blood vessels that supply blood to the heart. This disease includes angina and heart attack which share similar symptoms of pain or pressure in the chest. Unlike angina, the symptoms caused by heart attack do not subside with rest and may cause permanent damage to the heart. Smoking, lack of exercise, excess weight, high cholesterol levels in the blood, family history and high blood pressure are some of the factors that may contribute to this disease.

Heart Failure - is a condition in which the heart is unable to cope with its work load of pumping blood to the lungs and the rest of the body. The most common cause is severe coronary artery disease. The main symptoms are shortness of breath and swelling of the ankles and feet.

Heart-Rhythm Problems - are irregular or abnormal rhythms of the heart beat. In some cases heart-rhythm problems are caused by coroneary artery disease. Symptoms of heart-rhythm problems influttering in the chest (palpitation) and feeling light-headed. Some heart-rhythm problems are life-threatening and need emergency treatment.

Pyramid of Health Effects

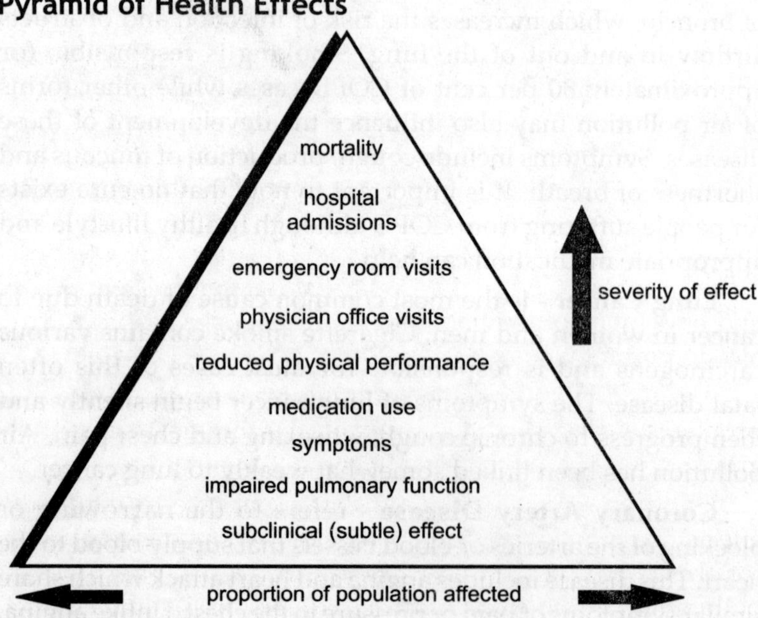

Air pollution can affect both the respiratory and cardiac systems. The health effects of air pollution can be seen as a pyramid, with the mildest but not common effects at the bottom of the pyramid and the least common but more severe at the top of the pyramid. The pyramid demonstrates that as severity decreases the number of people affected increases.

Health Endpoints Associated with Increased Air Pollutants Levels

Mortality: All non-accidental mortality causes.

Hospital Admissions: Cardiovascular and Respiratory Hospital Admissions.

Emergency Room Visits: Visit to an emergency department.

Asthma Symptom Days: Exacerbation of asthma symptoms in individuals with diagnosed asthma.

Restricted Activity Days: Days spent in bed, missed from work and days when activities are partially restricted due to illness.

Acute Respiratory Symptoms: Respiratory-related symptoms such as chest discomfort, coughing and wheezing.

Population at Risk

Although everyone is at risk from the health effects of air pollution, certain sub-populations are more susceptible. Individual reactions to air contaminants depend on several factors such as the type of pollutant, the degree of exposure and how much of the pollutant is present. Age and health are also important factors.

The elderly and people suffering from cardio-respiratory problems such as asthma appear to be the most susceptible groups.

Children and newborns are also sensitive to the health effects of air pollution since they take in more air than adults for their body weight and consequently, a higher level of pollutants. People who exercise outdoors on hot and smoggy days are also at greater risk due to their increased exposure to pollutants in the air.

Leading Causes of Hospitalization

Respiratory and cardiovascular diseases are among the leading causes of hospitalization in Canada. In 1996-1997 there were 3.16 million hospital admissions in Canada of which cardiovascular and respiratory diseases accounted for 15 per cent and 9 per cent, respectively.

Leading Causes of Hospitalization : Number and Percentage of Separation by Subgroup Canada 96-97

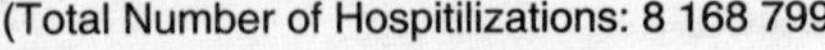
(Total Number of Hospitilizations: 8 168 799

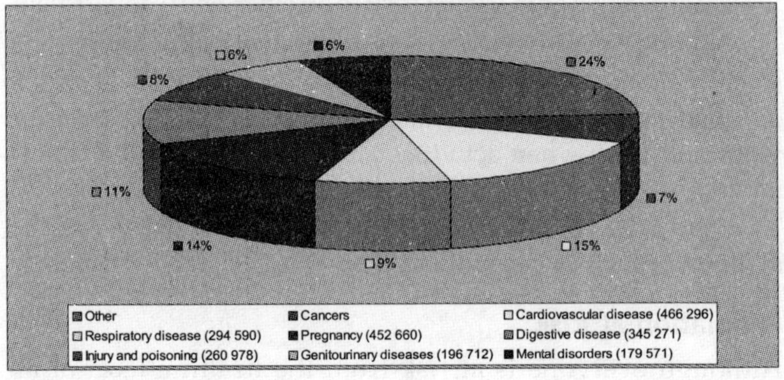

Source: Statistics Canada, 1999

Air pollution exacerbates the condition of people with respiratory and cardiovascular diseases and causes measurable increases in the rates of hospitalization for these diseases. We do not yet understand the role of air pollution in causing these illnesses in the Canadian population.

Leading Causes of Death

Cardiovascular and respiratory diseases are among the leading causes of death in Canada. In 1997, 37 per cent and 9 per cent of over 200000 deaths were related to cardiovascular and respiratory diseases respectively.

Air pollution causes measurable increases in non-accidental mortality.

Leading Causes of Death Number and Percentage of Deaths, Canada 199T

(Total number of deaths in 1997: 215 669)

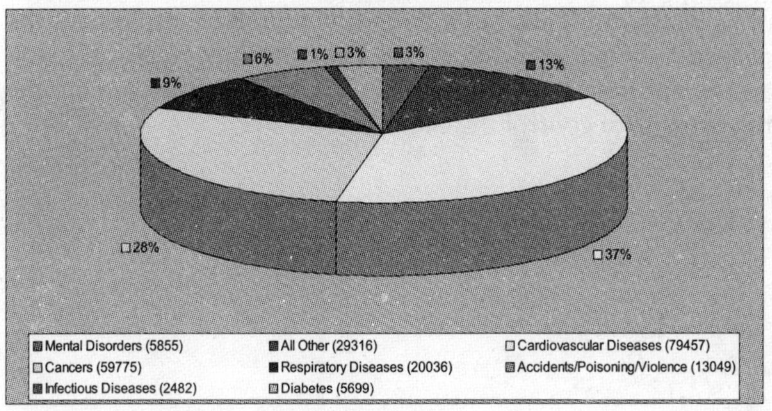

Source: Statistics Canada, 1999

Estimating Health Benefits

When examining a specific pollution-reduction option (such as changing gasoline composition) regulators may estimate the reduction in health effects that are expected and the value to society of avoiding those health problems.

As a society, we pay for the health effects of air pollution in many ways. Additional health care costs for the treatment of these effects may come from any of the following: hospital admissions, visits to the emergency room or doctor's office, homecare service, medication such as inhalers for asthma. Other considerations include lost productivity in the wsorkplace, lost wages due to sick time, out of pocket expenses incurred while ill (*e.g.*, additional child care costs), and finally lost quality of life or life itself.

Conclusion

A recent study examined the economic value of reducing the health effects of air pollution by introducing cleaner vehicles and fuels in Canada. This study found that the economic value of avoiding these health effects was $24 billion over a period of 24 years, compared to a cost of $6 billion to implement the program. This methodology has been used by Health Canada and Environment Canada in a number of initiatives to examine the benefits of control measures.

Air Pollution
Its Impacts on Air Quality

M.R. Jyothi Fedric
Principal
Government Degree College
Narasannapeta, Srikalum District, A.P.

Introduction

In a water resources project, air pollution occurs mainly during project construction phase. The major sources of air pollution during construction phase are:

- Fuel combustion in various construction equipment, *e.g.* crushers, drillers, rock bolters, diesel generating vehicles, etc.
- Fugitive emissions from crusher.
- Impacts due to vehicular movement.

Types

Pollution due to Fuel Combustion in Various Equipment

The operation of various construction equipment requires of combustion of fuel. Normally, diesel is used in such equipment. The major pollutant, which gets emitted as a result of diesel combustion, is SO_2. The SPM emissions are minimal due to low ash content. Based on past experience in similar projects, SPM and SO_2 are not expected to increase significantly. Thus, in the proposed project, no significant impact on ambient air quality is expected as a result of operation of various construction equipment.

Emissions from Crusher

The operation of the crusher during the construction phase is likely to generate fugitive emissions, which can move even up to 1 km in predominant wind direction. During construction phase, one crusher of 60 tph capacity is likely to be commissioned. During'crushing operations, fugitive emissions comprising of the suspended particulate will be generated. There could be marginal impacts to settlements close to the sites at which crusher is commissioned. However, based on past experience, adverse impacts on this account are not anticipated. However, during finalizing the project layout, it should be ensured that the labour camps, colonies, etc. are located on the leeward side and outside the impact zone (about 1.5 to 2 km) of the crushers.

Impacts due to Vehicular Movement

During construction phase, there will be increased vehicular movement for transportation of various construction materials to the project site. Large quantity of dust is likely to be entrained due to the movement of trucks and other heavy vehicles. However, such ground level emissions do not travel for long distances. Thus, no major adverse impacts are anticipated on this account.

Mitigation Measures

Control of Emissions: Minor air quality impacts will be caused by emissions from construction vehicles, equipment and DG sets and emissions from transportation traffic. Frequent truck trips will be required during the construction period for removal of excavated material and delivery of select concrete and other equipment and materials. The following measures are recommended to control air pollution:

- The contractor will be responsible for maintaining properly functioning construction equipment to minimize exhaust.
- Construction equipment and vehicles will be turned off when not used for extended periods of time.

- Unnecessary idling of construction vehicles to be prohibited.
- Effective traffic management to be undertaken to avoid significant delays in and around the project area.
- Road damage caused by sub-project activities will be promptly attended to with proper road repair and maintenance work.

Air Pollution control due to DG sets: The Central Pollution Control Board (CPCB) has issued emission limits for generators upto 800 kW. The same are outlined in Table 8.1 and are recommended to be followed.

Table 8.1 : Emission Limits for DG Sets Prescribed by CPCB

Parameter	Emission limits (gw/kWhr)
NO_x	9.2
HC	1.3
CO	2.5
PM	0.3
Smoke limit*	0.7

Note: Light-absorption coefficient at full load (m^{-1})

The above standards needs to followed by the contractor operating the DG sets. The other measures are recommended as below:

- Location of DG sets and other emission generating equipment should be decided keeping in view the predominant wind direction so that emissions do not effect nearby residential areas.
- Stack height of DG sets to be kept in accordance with CPCB norms, which prescribes the minimum height of stack to be provided with each generator set to be calculated using the following formula:

$$H = h + 0.2x \sqrt{kVA}$$

H = Total height of stack in metres

h = Height of the building in metres where the generator set is installed

kVA = Total generator capacity of the set in kVA

Dust Control: The project authorities will work closely with representatives from the community living in the vicinity of project area to identify areas of concern and to mitigate dust-related impacts effectively (*e.g.*, through direct meetings, utilization of construction management and inspection program, and/or through the complaint response programme). To minimize issues related to the generation of dust during the construction phase of the project, the following measures have been identified:

- Identification of construction limits (minimal area required for construction activities).
- When practical, excavated spoils will be removed as the contractor proceeds along the length of the activity.
- When necessary, stockpiling of excavated material will be covered or staged offsite location with muck being delivered as needed during the course of construction.
- Excessive soil on paved areas will be sprayed (wet) and/or swept and unpaved areas will be sprayed and/or mulched. The use of petroleum products or similar products for such activities will be strictly prohibited.
- Contractors will be required to cover stockpiled soils and trucks hauling soil, sand and other loose materials (or require trucks to maintain at least two feet of freeboard).
- Contractor shall ensure that there is effective traffic management at site. The number of trucks/vehicles to move at various construction sites to be fixed.
- Dust sweeping - The construction area and vicinity (access roads, and working areas) shall be swept with water sweepers on a daily basis or as necessary to ensure there is no visible dust.

Conclusion

Various management measures needs to be implemented for Control of air pollution control need to be included in the Tender Document for the Contractor involved in construction activities. The same shall be monitored on a regular basis by the project proponents.

Impact of Women Education on Environment in India

Akankshya Patnaik
Assistant Professor
Presidency College, Berhampur

Introduction

The shifting of the emphasis from the tradition towards modernity will present a different picture and after scenario will speak the dilemma of the common people. The status of women was somehow equal in ancient times. In spite of the strong and determined march towards the commitment of the changing generation we can conclude that - Future of India is still doubtful talking about women.

As per the view of many scholars our ancient times women power was very much accepted in the society. As per the previous record of ancient Indian grammarist *Patanjali and Katyayana* suggest that women were educated in early *Vedic period.* Scriptures like *Rig-Veda* and *Upanishad* given light on several women sages, identifying *Gargi and Maitreyi.*

But in the change of time the women power and prestige slowly vanished. With the approach of medial age different ghastly systems like *sati, child marriage,* and *ban on widow marriage* raise their head firmly. In which women education and employment concepts became smoke in fire. In this time women remain as a working poppet in the hand of cruel man folk. In spite of all these odds and obstacles some women could prove them self in the field of politics, literature, education & religion. *Razia Sultana* the only woman monarch who ruled Delhi, Gond queen *Durgavati* rule for 15 years before losing her life in battle, *Nur Jehan* wielded imperial power behind the thorne, Mugal princess *Zahanara & Zebunnissa* were well known poets & *Mirabai* a female saint who had proved their worth.

Women played an important role in modern India. She could able to participate in India's freedom Struggle. *Sister Nivedita, Jhansi Rani Laxmi Bai, Sarojini Naidu* could able to write their name in golden letters in Indian history. Slowly India could recognise the extraordinary roll of women *Indira Gandhi* as Iron women of India, *Kalpana Chcrwla* 1st woman in space, Mother of mothers *Mother Teresa.*

The early 1970's the emphasis on women empowerment & their connection with environment was noted with reference to the book entitled *"Woman's Role in Economic Development"* written by *Esther Boserup*. The Women, Environment & Development debate (WED) began in early 1970's.

In Mexico City (1975) at the first world conference on women. *Vandana Shiva* introduced the issue of women & the environment. *Vandana Shiva* has pointed out different issues for bringing *ecofeminism* into public or social consciousness by her report on Chipko movement. ***Ecofeminism*** concept says that women are closer to nature then men. This closeness therefore makes women more nurturing and caring towards their environment. She has presented *Women* in a unique way by stating that relationship with the land and other natural resources. We can call it *Crazy Fabrics* means women has close affinity with nature or environment. The Indian women universally promote the new culture of respect towards the preservation and use of natural resources and environment.

Starting from 1980's, policy maker and government were very careful & mindful regarding women and environment.

At the outside of time the Indian women present a signal to aware the common people to become conscious about the global trends. They are working together to create awareness and fight against economic dilemmas. They have created the special value system to fight against environmental issues. Both women & nature have been considered as subordinate entities throughout history, which conveys close relationship between them. If we go through the history it is commonly understood that men have utilized natural resources as commercial entities or income generating tools, while women have tendered to see the environment as resource supporting their basic needs.

With the roll of time Indian social worker & government joined their hand to bring reform. 1990's the formation of new women oriented NGO *(SEWA) Self-Employed Women Association* is a bright example of social & environmental reformation. *2001* was declared by Indian government as the *year of women empowerment.* Our Indian Constitution also joined his hand in this progress chapter of women.

The Constitution of India guarantees to all Indian *women equality* (Article 14), *no discrimination* by the State (Article 15(1)), *equality of opportunity* (Article 16), and *equal pay for equal work* (Article 39(d)). In addition, it allows special provisions to be made by the State *in favour of women and children* (Article 15(3)), renounces practices derogatory to the dignity of women (Article 51 (A) (e)), and also allows for provisions to be made by the State for securing just and *humane conditions of work and for maternity relief* (Article 42).

Woman Education

Education is a key part of strategies to improve individuals' well-being and societies'. Although in Vedic period the women were in access to education. But with the pass of time the women education was buried under the man dominated society. With the emerge of British period slowly women power raise its head & again women education came to the face. Record shows that in 1971 only 22 per cent women were literate by the end of 2001 the literacy rate could able to touch 54.16 per cent. But if we see 2001 census we can find male literacy rate is more than 75 per cent compared to female literacy rate which is just 54.16 per cent. We can see the changing rate of literacy in India from Table 9.1 below.

Table 9.1 : Literacy Rate in India (1901-2011)

Year	Persons	Males	Females
1901	5.3	9.8	0.7
1911	5.9	10.6	1.1
1921	7.2	12.2	1.8
1931	9.5	15.6	2.9
1941	16.1	24.9	7.3
1951	16.7	24.9	7.3
1961	24.0	34.4	13.0
1971	29.5	39.5	18.7
1981	36.2	46.9	24.8
1991	52.1	63.9	39.2
2001	65.38	76.0	54.0
2011	74.04	82.14	65.46

Source: Census of India (2011).

Literacy Rate in India

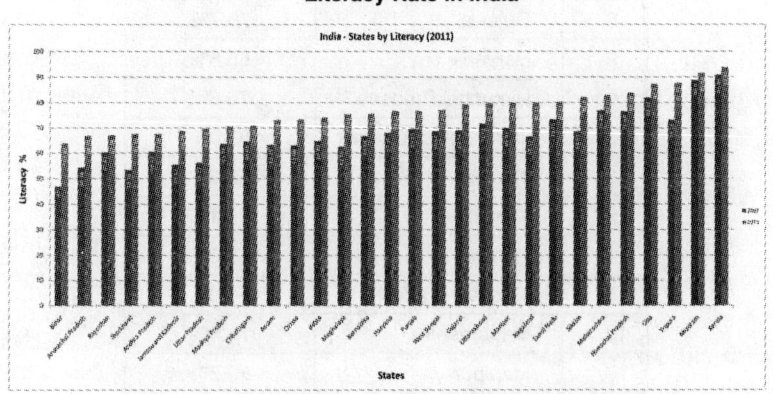

2011 census report says that literacy rate of women before independence were very poor, but if we see the data at the time of independence we can see the sharp rise of female literacy from 0.7 to 7.3 per cent. It is really surprising to note that the faster pace of female literacy surpass male literacy during the decade 1981 to 2001. But today also we can note from various surveys that school dropouts are more in case of female & numbers of female are least in higher education.

If we will minutely notice the changes in female literate rate we can find an uneven growth rate in whole country. Table 9.2 below shows the female literacy as per 2011 census survey report.

Table 9.2 : State-wise Percentage of Female Literacy as Per 2011 Census Report

Sl. No.	Name of the State	Female Literacy
1.	Andhra Pradesh	59.7%
2.	Arunachal Pradesh	59.6%
3.	Assam	67.3%
4.	Bihar	53.3%
5.	Chhattisgarh	60.6%
6.	Delhi	80.9%
7.	Goa	81.8%
8.	Gujarat	70.7%
9.	Haryana	66.8%
10.	Himachal Pradesh	76.6%
11.	Jammu and Kashmir	58.0%
12.	Jharkhand	56.2%
13.	Karnataka	68.1%
14.	Kerala	92.0%
15.	Madhya Pradesh	60.0%
16.	Maharashtra	75.5%
17.	Manipur	73.2%

18.	Meghalaya	73.8%
19.	Mizoram	89.4%
20.	Nagaland	76.7%
21.	Orissa	64.4%
22.	Punjab	71.3%
23.	Rajasthan	52.7%
24.	Sikkim	76.4%
25.	Tamil Nadu	73.9%
26.	Tripura	83.1%
27.	Uttar Pradesh	59.3%
28.	Uttarakhand	70.7%
29.	West Bengal	71.2%
Union Territories		
1.	Andaman & Nicobar Islands	81.8%
2.	Chandigarh	81.4%
3.	Dadra & Nagar Haveli	65.9%
4.	Daman & Diu	79.6%
5.	Lakshadweep	88.2%
6.	Pondicherry	81.2%
	All India	**65.46%**

Source: Census of India - 2011

From the report above we can easily know that many States are still below average that is 60 per cent. Irregular distribution can be observed clearly from the survey, where Kerala touches 92.0 per cent & being able to be in the top of female literacy rate at the same time Rajasthan could manage to get only 52.7 per cent and take its position in the bottom of growth ladder. In Rajasthan, less than 12 per cent of rural women are literate. In 6 of the 24 States, 25 per cent or less of the women in rural areas is literate. It is true that the women empowerment programme, related policies & norms, reservation, etc are planned, but not implemented in full fledge. If we can implement those plans in full fledge then with surety we can say that future of the India would be really bright.

Woman Education—Socio-cultural Environment

Women are undoubtly the foundation of the basic unit of society - *the family,* which is clear from the view *of Pt. Jawaharlal Nehru:* 'If you educate a man you educate an individual, however, if you educate a woman you educate a whole family."

Women empowered means mother India empowered. Education helps women to give a better life to their children & contributing for the right career decision. Not only this but also it could help her father, brother & husband in their business, job & financial decisions. Educated women can develop the quality of life of inside & outside their home. As per various survey it is noticed that women make-up 66 per cent of world's literate adults. Female literacy could able to reduce the dowry & brutal killing of brides in India which is a headline issue in every day new paper. Educated women could able to face the challenges like sexual harassment & exploitation and could able to take the right step when needed. More over education helps women in reducing infant mortality rate & growth of population.

Woman Education - Economic Environment

Across the world, educated & empowered women has proven time & again to be the catalyst for rapid economic growth of the country. This is very much clear from the view point of Napoleon, the great conqueror of his times, ***"Give me good Mother; I will give you good Nation".*** Going back to history we can witness the multiple roles of women in various fields. They could able to show their extraordinary ability, skills, intelligence, hard work & sincerity, innovation, care & commitment in nation building. If we harness this attribute properly then we can witness a better tomorrow. The education of women is the key for all success and betterment.

Conclusion

From this study it is clear that Indian education system is growing & we can also notice the growth of female literacy. But, its slow pace can't make many changes in socio-economic development of our country. Society & government are doing their best. No one can bring the change without our effort. Let's start the revolution within our self to improve the condition of women, our family, our socio-economic environment, our State & more over our country.

REFERENCES

1. A Search for Aggregate-Level Effects of Education on Fertility, Using Data from Zimbabwe Qystein Kravdal © 2000 Max-Planck-Gesellschaft ISSN 1435-9871.
2. Farzaneh Roudi-Fahimi and Valentine M. Moghadam, *Empowering Women, Developing Society: Female Education in the Middle East and North Africa.*
3. From Wikipedia, the free encoclopaedia
4. Government of India, Census of India 2001.
5. Gupta, N.L. (2003) *Women's Education Through Ages*, Concept Publishing Co, New Delhi.
6. *Helpdesk Research Report* (2009): The Impact of Conflict on Women's Education, Employment and Health Care, Government & Social Development Research Centre
7. Prema, A. (2012), *Women Status in India*, Vol. 2 Issue 1, Indian Streams Research Journal
8. Rao, R.K. (2001) *Women and Education*, Kalpaz Publications, Delhi.
9. Report on the online discussion on gender, education and employment (2010)
10. S.P., Agarwal (200l), *Women's Education in India (1995-98) Present Status, Perspective, Plan, Statistical Indicators with Global View*, Vol. III Concept Publishing Co, New Delhi.

11. Sharmila, N. and Albert Christopher Dhas (2010), *Development of Women Education in India*, MPRA Paper No. 20680
12. Suguna, M. (2011) *Education and Women Empowerment in India*, Vol. 1, Issue 8, ZENITH International Journal of Multidisciplinary Research, ISSN 2231 5780
13. Velkoff, Victoria A. (1998), *Women's Education in India,* Women of the World
14. "Women and the Environment" From Wikipedia, the free encyclopaedia

10

Environmental Pollution Impact on the Indian Economy

Dr. D. Tatarao
Reader in Commerce, Government Degree College, Yelamanchili, Visakhapatnam District, Andhra Pradesh

Introduction

The environmental pollution affect the health of more than 100 million people worldwide. Pollution is the contaminant into a natural environment, usually by humans. The specific types of pollution are land pollution, air pollution, water pollution (oceans, rivers, ground water), Plastic pollution, Noise pollution, Light pollution, space Ozone layer and many more. In India the increasing economic development and a rapidly growing population that has taken the country from 300 million people in 1947 to more than one billion people today is putting a strain on the environment, infrastructure, and the country's natural resources. Industrial pollution, soil erosion, deforestation, rapid-industrialization, urbanization, and land degradation are all worsening problems. Overexploitation of the country's resources be it land or water and the industrialization process has resulted environmental degradation of resources. Environmental pollution is one of the most serious problems facing humanity and other life forms on our planet today.

India's per capita carbon dioxide emissions were roughly) 3,000 pounds (1,360 kilograms) in 2007, according to the study. That's small compared to China and the U.S., with 10,500 pounds (4.763 kilograms) and 42,500 pounds (19,278 kilograms) respectively that year. The study said that the European Union and Russia also have more emissions than India.

Types of Pollution

India is among the world's worst performers when it comes to the overall environment. We rank 125 of 132 countries. Even Pakistan and Bangladesh are less polluted than we are. A study released earlier this year by the environmental research centres of Columbia and Yale showed that India was at the bottom of the heap when it came to air pollution.

Coal Pollution: India's environmental problems are exacerbated by its heavy reliance on coal for power generation. "More than 80 per cent of energy is produced from coal, a fuel that emits a high amount of carbon and greenhouse gases" said Bikash. According to IMF chief Christine Lagarde on July 10, 2012 said pollution from coal generation plants causes about 70,000 premature deaths every year in India. Andhra Pradesh, the coastal State of eastern India is experiencing a coal-plant construction boom, including the 4,000-MW Krishnapatnam Ultra Mega Power Project, one of nine such massive projects in planning or under construction in country.

On August 23, 2011 the Jharkhand State Pollution Control Board has ordered the closure of 22 BCCL mines in the underground fire zone of Jharia. BCCL had taken over most of the 103 mines from private owners. Hence, none of them had got environmental clearances. Most of the coal mines under the JSPCB's scanner were located in Jharia.

The 2,640-MW Sompeta plant proposed by Nagarjuna Construction Company and the 2,640-MW Bhavanapadu plant proposed by East Coast Energy have both provoked large nonviolent protests that have ended in police attacks, including four deaths of local residents.

As of May 2011, the Sompeta plant had been cancelled and the Bhavanapadu plant had been placed on hold by officials, with corruption investigations continuing. On April 12, 2011 the Ministry of Environment and Forests (MoEF) has tightened pollution monitoring norms for power projects with a generation capacity of 500 MW and above, integrated steel plants with a capacity of 1 million tonnes per annum and cement plants with a capacity of 3 million tonnes per annum.

Polluting Industrial Units: On May 26, 2011 the Haryana State Pollution Control Board has ordered closure of 639 polluting industrial units in 2010-11 and directed the highly polluting industries to set up continuous online monitoring stations to ensure compliance of standards of air emissions. The Government has launched prosecution against 151 polluting units in the Special Environment Courts in Faridabad and Kurukshetra, and made 9,239 units install pollution control devices.

Brick Kilns are Noxious Sources of Pollution: India's 100,000 brick kilns are noxious sources of pollution, particularly soot, and working them means a life that is always nasty, frequently brutish and often short. But on top of this social evil is an environmental one.

The exhaust from the kilns mixes with diesel emissions and other fumes to form a vast brown smog, known as an atmospheric brown cloud, which is up to 3 km thick and thousands of kilometres long. Two of its main ingredients, the small carbon particles which the soot is composed of and ozone, a triatomic form of oxygen, are important contributors to the greenhouse effect and thus to climate change. Among other negative effects, the cloud is therefore thought to be accelerating the retreat of Himalayan glaciers, which are found at a similar altitiude.

Aircraft Pollutants: According to a study published in the journal Environmental Science and Technology (EST) in the first week of October 2010, almost 8,000 people will die due to aircraft pollutants this year, and 3,500 of them would be from India and China.

A recent report by MIT researchers says that the harmful pollutants emitted by an aircraft at an altitude of 35,000 ft are fatal for people. The report says that nitrogen and sulphur oxides emitted by aircraft at 35,000 ft combine with other gases in the atmosphere to create noxious particulate matter.

Vehicle Emissions are responsible for 70 per cent of the country's air pollution. The major problem with government efforts to safeguard the environment has been enforcement at the local level, not with a lack of laws. Air pollution from vehicle exhaust and industry is a worsening problem for India. Exhaust from vehicles has increased eight-fold over levels of twenty years ago; industrial pollution has risen four times over the same period. The economy has grown ftro and a half times over the past two decades but pollution control and civil services have not kept pace. Air quality is worst in big cities like Kolkata, Delhi, Mumbai, Chennai, etc. According to the Society of Indian Automobile Manufacturers, India's auto production has doubled from 7 million units in fiscal year 2004 to over 14 million units in year 2010 largely on the back of a buoyant domestic market.

Bangalore holds the title of being the asthma capital of the country. Air pollution in the city continues to rise due to vehicular emissions and dust from construction activities, according to the "Environment Report Card of Bangalore 2012". It says the number of vehicles on the city roads have exceeded 3.7 million and there has been a consistent increase in the number vehicles at an average of 8 per cent per year.

Chennai: Exhaust from vehicles, dust from construction debris, industrial waste, burning of municipal and garden waste are all on the rise in the city. So are respiratory diseases, including asthma. At least six of the 10 top causes of death are related to respiratory disease, says Dr. D. Ranganathan, Director (in-charge), Institute of Thoracic Medicine.

Mumbai: Not only are levels of Suspended Particulate Matter (SPM) above permissible limits in Mumbai, but the worst pollutant after vehicular emissions has grown at an alarming rate. The levels of Respirable Suspended Particulate Matter

(RSPM), or dust, in Mumbai's air have continued to increase over the past three years.

The air pollution in Mumbai is so high that Mumbai authorities have purchased 42,000 litres of perfume to spray on the city's enormous waste dumps at Deonar and Mulund landfill sites after people living near the landfill sites complained of the stench. The Deonar landfill site, one of India's largest, was first used by the British in 1927. Today, the festering pile covers more than 120 hectares and is eight storys high.

Bhopal: Bhopal gas tragedy was the greatest industrial disaster in the world that took place at a Union Carbide pesticide plant in the Indian city of Bhopal, Madhya Pradesh. At midnight on 3 December 1984, the plant accidentally released methyl isocyanate (MIC) gas, exposing more than 500,000 people to MIC and other chemicals. The first official immediate death toll was 2,259. The Government of Madhya Pradesh has confirmed a total of 3,787 deaths related to the gas release. Others estimate 8.000-10,000 died within 72 hours and 25,000 have since died from gas-related diseases, making it the deadliest man-made environmental disaster in history.

The effects of air pollution are obvious: rice crop yields in southern India are falling as brown clouds block out more and more sunlight. The brilliant white of the famous Taj Mahal is slowly fading to a sickly yellow. In the "Tajmahal Case" a very strong step was taken by Supreme Court to save the Tajmahal being polluted by fumes and more than 200 factories were closed down.

Birds and species affected: Studies conducted by the high altitude zoology field station of the Zoological Survey of India (ZSI) based in Solan town of Himachal Pradesh have recorded a drastic fall in butterfly numbers in the western Himalayas, famous for their biodiversity.

The population of 50 per cent of the 288 species recorded in the western Himalayas, Himachal Pradesh and Jammu and

Kashmir, have declined more than half in just 10 years according to **World Environment Day 2012.**

Indoor air pollution: Indoor air pollution is the most important cause of chronic obstructive pulmonary disease (COPD) in India, says a prevalence study conducted by Pune-based Chest Research Foundation (CRF) and the Imperial College, London in November 2010. Over 700 million people in India suffer from high levels of indoor air pollution affecting women and young children as 75 per cent homes use biomass fuel like wood, crop residue and dung cakes. The National Institute of Environmental Health Sciences (NIEHS) is working to understand how exposures to environmental agents trigger diseases such as Asthma, and these diseases can be prevented, diagnosed and treated. Additionally, the NIEHS is developing and testing new technologies to help determine environmental triggers and reduce asthma symptoms.

Air Pollution

India has the worst air pollution in the entire world, beating China, Pakistan, Nepal and Bangladesh, according to a study released during this year's World Economic Forum in Davos. Of 132 countries whose environments were surveyed, India ranks dead last in the 'Air (effects on human health)' ranking. The annual study, the Environmental Performance Index, is conducted and written by environmental research centres at Yale and Columbia universities with assistance from dozens of outside scientists. The study uses satellite data to measure air pollution concentrations.

The World Health Organization estimates that about two million people die prematurely every year as a result of Air pollution, while many more suffer from breathing ailments, heart disease, lung infections and even cancer. Fine particles or microscopic dust from coal or wood fires and unfiltered diesel engines are rated as one of the most lethal forms or air pollution caused by industry, transport, household heating, cooking and ageing coal or oil-fired power stations.

There are four reasons of air pollution are - emissions from vehicles, thermal power plants, industries and refineries. The problem of indoor air pollution in rural areas and urban slums has increased.

CNG is not without environmental drawbacks says a new Central Pollution Control Board study on January 05, 2011. The study says burning CNG has the highest rates of potentially hazardous carbonyl emissions. The study also made a case for regulating CNG and other fuels for methane emissions. Methane, a greenhouse gas, is a key contributor to *climate change.* Among the study's finds were that retrofitted CNG car engines emit 30 per cent more methane than original CNG engines. Almost all CNG car engines in India are retrofitted.

One major study in September 2011 found that components of diesel exhaust including particulate matter can cause biologic responses that are related to Asthma this exposure is associated with the inflammatory and immune responses involved in asthma.

Studies conducted in various parts of the world have revealed a strong link between type 2 diabetes and cardiovascular diseases and continuous exposure to ultra fine particulate matter present in the air. Particluate matter in the air which is very fine and is less than 2.5 microns in size is called PM 2.5 and has been known to cause diabetes and cardiovascular diseases.

Indian air pollution has been blamed for its dry monsoon season, but a scientist has revealed that European pollution may also play a part in it. The volume of the summer monsoon has been weakening since the 1950s. And Yi Ming of Princeton University in New Jersey claimed his experimental models suggest that the effect of European aerosol pollution accounts for about half the drop in the volume of monsoon rainfall - the other half is down to pollution over south Asia.

River Water Pollution

Contaminated and polluted water now kills more people than all forms of violence including wars, according to a United Nations report released on March 22, 2010 on World Water Day that calls for turning unsanitary wastewater into an environmentally safe economic resource. According to the report titled "Sick Water?" 90 per cent of wastewater discharged daily in developing countries is untreated, contributing to the deaths of some 2.2 million people a year from diarrheal diseases caused by unsafe drinking water and poor hygiene. At least 1.8 million children younger than 5 die every year from water-related diseases.

Fully 80 per cent of urban waste in India ends up in the country's rivers and unchecked urban growth across the country combined with poor government oversight means the problem is only getting worse. A growing number of bodies of water in India are unfit for human use,' and in the *River Ganga*, holy to the country's 82 per cent Hindu majority, is dying slowly due to unchecked pollution. New Delhi's body of water is little more than a flowing garbage dump, with fully 57 per cent of the city's waste finding its way to the Yamuna. It is that three billion liters of waste are pumped into Delhi's Yamuna (River Yamuna) each day. Only 55 per cent of the 15 million Delhi residents are connected to the city's sewage system. The remainder flush their bath water, waste water and just about everything else down pipes and into drains, most of them empty into the Yamuna. According to the Centre for Science and Environment, between 75 and 80 per cent of the river's pollution is the result of raw sewage. Combined with industrial runoff, the garbage thrown into the river and it totals over 3 billion liters of waste per day. Nearly 20 billion rupees, or almost US $S500 million, has been spent on various clean up efforts.

The Frothy Brew is so Glaring that it can be viewed on Google Earth

Much of the river pollution problem in India comes from untreated sewage. Samples taken recently from the Ganges River near Varanasi show that levels of fecal coliform, a dangerous bacterium that comes from untreated sewage, were some 3,000 per cent higher than what is considered safe for bathing.

Groundwater Exploitation

Groundwater exploitation is a serious matter of concern today and legislations and policy measures taken till date, by the state governments (water is a state subject) have not had the desired effect on the situation.

Groundwater Quality and Pollution is most alarming pollution hazards in India. On April 01, 2010 at least 18 babies in several hamlets of Bihar's Bhojpur district have been born blind in the past three months because their families consume groundwater containing alarming levels of arsenic, confirmed by Bihar's Health Minister Nand Kishore Yadav on Wednesday, 31st March 2010 confirmed the cases of blindness in newborns in arsenic caffected blocks of the district.

According to the World Health Organization on *World Water Day 2012*. on March 22 each year, an estimated four billion people get sick with diarrhoea as a result of drinking unsafe water, inadequate sanitation, and poor hygiene. Nearly two million people die from diarrhoea each year and many of them children under the age of five, poor and living in the developing world. Improper disposal of solid waste, both by the public and Bruhat Bangalore Mahanagara Palike (BBMP) is causing direct contamination of groundwater, according to Dr M A Farooqui, scientist, Central Ground Water Board (CGWB).

Plastic Pollution

Plastic bags, plastic thin sheets and plastic waste is also a major source of pollution. A division bench of Allahabad High Court, comprising Justice Ashok Bhushan and Justice Arun Tandon, in May 03, 2010 had directed the Ganga Basin Authority and the state government to take appropriate action to ban the use of polythene in the vicinity of Ganga in the entire State. Also *Plastic Bag Pollution in the country* is one of the biggest hazards. On August 2, 2010, seeking to know whether a fine should be imposed on *paan masala* or *gutkha* packet manufacturers for polluting and choking the drainage systems, the Supreme Court has directed the Union Government to file its reply in six weeks.

From January 20, 2011 sale of plastic or polythene bags has been banned in the vicinity of rivers or any other'water body after Uttar Pradesh Governor B. L. Joshi gave his assent to an ordinance in this regard. "The Governor has given his assent to UP Plastic and Bio-Degradable Garbage and Waste (Use and Disposal) Ordinance which makes areas around river and water bodies no-polythene zone," he said.

Municipal Solid Waste

India's urban population slated to increase from the current 330 million to about 600 million by 2030, the challenge of managing municipal solid waste (MSW) in an environmentally and economically sustainable manner is bound to assume gigantic proportions . The country has over 5,000 cities and towns, which generate about 40 million tonnes of MSW per year today. Going by estimates of The Energy Research Institute (TERI), this could well touch 260 million tonnes per year by 2047.

Municipal solid waste is solid waste generated by households, commercial establishments and offices does not include the industrial or agricultural waste. Municipal solid waste management is more of an administrative and institutional mechanism failure problem rather than a technological one. Until now, MSW management has been considered to be almost the sole responsibility of urban governments, without the participation of citizens and other stakeholders. The Centre and the Supreme Court, however, have urged that this issue be addressed with multiple stakeholder participation. Cities in India spend approximately 20 per cent of the city budget on solid waste services.

Pollution due to Mining

New Delhi-based Center for Science and Environment (CSE) on December 29, 2007 said mining was causing displacement, pollution, forest degradation and social unrest. According to the Centre for Science and Environment (CSE) report the top 50 mineral producing districts, as many as 34 fall under the 150 most backward districts identified in the country. The CSE report has made extensive analysis of environment degradation and pollution due to mining, wherein it has said, in 2005-06 alone 1.6 billion tonnes of waste and overburden from coal, iron ore, limestone and bauxite have added to environment pollution. With the annual growth of mining at 10.7 per cent and 500-odd mines awaiting approval of the Centre, the pollution would increase manifold in the coming years.

The mines of Mahanadi Coal Fields and NTPC draw about 25 Cr litres of water per day from the River Brahmani and in return they release thousands of gallons of waste water, which contains obnoxious substances like Ash, Oil, Heavy Metals, Grease, Fluorides, Phosphorus, Ammonia, Urea and Sulphuric Acid, into the River Nandira (A tributary of River Brahmani). The effluents from chlorine plant cause chloride and sodium toxicity to the river Rushikulya—the lifeline of southern Odisha. The Phosphoric Fertilizer Industry discharges effluent containing Nitric, Sulphuric and Phosphoric acids into river Mahanadi. ToI reported on March 2, 2012 that in Goa the open cast extraction of iron ore has created a degraded environment with several resultant ills of air and groundwater pollution and severe social impacts. Environmentalists say that severe damage

to the state's verdant landscape in the form of deforestation, ground and surface water pollution and damage to agricultural land and beaches in a worrisome area of concern.

The Supreme Court on February 25, 2011 ordered a probe by its committee into alleged illegal mining in Bellary and other forest areas of Karnataka. A bench headed by Chief Justice S.H. Kapadia asked the apex court – appointed Central Empowered Committee to conduct the probe and file its report within six weeks.

The explosive report of Lokayukta on July 28, 2011 uncovered major violations and systemic corruption in mining in Bellary Environmental degradation in this region in terms of plundering forest land and complete violation of air and water pollution standards have been devastating. Due to illegal mining in Bellary tanks and natural streams are polluted. There is evidence of perennial rivers drying up and complete devastation of roads and other infrastructure due to transportation of iron ore.

Despite stone mining's links to several occupational diseases such as pneumoconiosis, silicosis, tuberculosis, asbestosis and asthma, abject poverty keeps driving villagers in many parts of the Rajasthan State to illegal mining. Rajasthan is the largest producer of dimensional stones in the country. The state produces 5 crore tonnes a year.

An aluminum refinery in Odisha blithely continues to pollute the surrounding villages, despite the recommendations of the Supreme Court's Central Empowered Committee that it be closed since it poses environmental and health hazards. Rengopalli in the east and west cells of the Red Mud pond built for the refinery's alkaline waste disposal. Red Mud, which is the final waste product from bauxite. In the currently operational west cell, a tonne of toxic waste is dumped for every ton of alumina produced in the refinery.

In Jharkhand there are abundant coalmines, most of the coalmines are situated in Hazaribagh, Chatra, Palamau,

Rajmahal, Dhanbad and Ranchi district. Mighty Damodar River and its tributaries flow through these coalmines. Due to extensive coal mining and vigorous growth of industries in this area water resources have been contaminated.

Thousands of villagers in Odisha are facing serious health risks as a "cocktail of toxic residue" leaks from an aluminium refinery, Amnesty International warned June 1, 2011. Amnesty said it has video footage showing toxic residue spilling onto the roads from the main red mud pond of the Vedanta Aluminium Refinery.

Due to *large scale illegal mining in India* and in *The Aravalli hills Range in Raiasthan* and Haryana the forest cover has been depicted 90 per cent and drying up wells and affecting agriculture. The governments remain silent in these years. Due to media and public protest the Supreme Court on February 20, 2010 directed cancellation of 157 mining leases operating in Rajasthan's eco-sensitive Aravalli Hills. On August 24, 2010 the Ministry of Environment and Forest (MoEF) has rejected permission for the Anil Agarwal promoted Vedanta mining project in Odisha. In a statement, the ministry has said that "the forest clearance for Vedanta stands rejected".

The Saxena committee report accused the Vedanta smelters in Odisha, including the Posco Integrated Steel project in Odisha, which, at ₹ 56,000 crore is the single-largest foreign direct investment in India, the Jindal Thermal Power Plant in Chhattisgarh (₹ 10,000 crore), hydroelectric projects on Bhagirathi in Uttarakhand and the Navi Mumbai airport in Maharashtra (₹ 7,972 crore).

Pollution due to Biomedical Waste

Pollution due to biomedical waste is likely to spread diseases which are dangerous to life and making atmosphere noxious to health. In early April, 2010 a machine from Delhi University containing cobalt-60, a radioactive metal used for radiotherapy in hospitals, ended up in a scrap yard in the city. The death from radiation poisoning of a scrap yard worker in *Delhi* has highlighted the lax enforcement of waste disposal laws in India. The International Atomic Energy Agency said it was the worst radiation incident worldwide in four years.

India being used as a dumping ground for hazardous waste, from foreign countries. Twenty containers with goods were detained by the officials of Special Intelligence and Investigation Branch attached to the Customs Department here recently. Packs of broken toys, used diapers, empty perfume bottles, used battery cells, thermocol, used aluminum foil packing materials and coloured surgical gloves were found in the containers. It could also lead to contamination and spread of communicable diseases.

Pollution due to e-Waste

A UN Environmental Conference in Cartagena, Colombia, attended by more than 170 countries in October 2011, has agreed to accelerate a global ban on the export of hazardous waste, including old electronics and discarded computers and mobile phones, from developed to developing countries. Environmental campaigners, who have been battling to broker a deal on the dumping of toxic waste for more than 20 years, said they were "ecstatic" about this "major breakthrough". "All forms of hazardous waste including that sent for recycling, to obsolete electronic waste, will be banned from leaving wealthy countries destined for developing countries."

The UNEP report "Recycling from E-Waste to Resources" was released on the Indonesian island of Bali on February 22, 2010 at the start of a week-long meeting of officials and environmentalists. According to the report's authors by 2020 e-waste in South Africa and China will have jumped by 200-400 per cent from 2007 levels and by 500 per cent in India.

India produces about 3,80,000 tonnes of e-Waste per annum, which includes only the waste generated out of television sets, mobile phones and PCs, a major chunk of which comes from organizations. E-waste produced in India includes over 100,000 tonnes from refrigerators, 275,000 tonnes from TVs, 56.300 tonnes from personal computers, 4,700 tonnes from printers and 1,700 tonnes from mobile phones. The unorganized recycling sector which fails to practice eco-friendly e-Waste recycling methods release large amount of toxic chemicals. The toxic gases and the large volume of *Electronic Waste Adds environmental Pollution in* India.

India imports almost 50.000 tonnes of e-waste yearly. It generated 330,000 tonnes of e-waste in 2007 and the number is expected to touch 470,000 tonnes by 2011. According to a study on e-waste assessment conducted jointly by MAIT and the German government's sustainable development body GTZ. in April 2010.

Noise Pollution

Noise pollution is a type of atmospheric pollution. It constitutes a real and present danger to people's health and can produce serious physical and psychological stress. Researches have proved that a loud noise during peak marketing hours creates tiredness, irritation and impairs brain activities so as to reduce thinking and working abilities. It affects sleep, hearing, communication, mental and physical health. It may even lead to the madness of people. High noise levels can contribute to cardiovascular effects in humans, a rise in blood pressure, and an increased incidence of coronary artery disease. In animals also noise can increase the risk of death by altering predator, interfere with reproduction and navigation, and contribute to permanent hearing loss.

A paper by federal scientists and Cornell University researchers published in October 2012 estimates that in the last 50 years, the area where the whales can effectively communicate in Stellwagen Bank and surrounding waters off Massachusetts has fallen by two-thirds because of the noise.

The main source of noise pollution are automobiles, loudspeakers, firecrackers burst during festivals, industries, low-flying aircrafts, In India there is Noise Pollution Control Rule 2000 uader Environment Protection Act 1996.

Delhi's Air is Choking with Pollutant PM 2.5

The CSE report claimed that Delhi are's air reeling under concoction of pollutants like nitrogen and carbon monoxide (CO). Patients complaining of chest and throat infections have shot up in the past two weeks. Experts have blamed high pollution levels in the capital for this.

Delhi's air is choking with pollutant PM 2.5 that is only 2.5 microns in diameter and is very very small particle. Being so small, it escapes emission apparatus prescribed by Euro II and III. Any" kind of combustion, especially of vehicular origin, contains this particle. If PM 2.5 is not regulated it will ensure major health hazards. The number of Asthma patients will rise and in future there may huge rise of lung cancer cases also. The toxic value of PM 2.5 is such that metals like lead present in the PM 2.5 get inhaled deeper into lungs which deposits there.

The children are most affected by depositing lead due to inhaling the poisonous air. The increasing amount of PM 2.5 is like a poison in the air we breathe. Toxic smog is set to engulf Delhi once again this winter after a six-year respite because of the huge number of new cars clogging the roads. New Delhi adds nearly 1,000 new cars a day to the existing four million registered in the city, almost twice as many as before 2000. Pollution levels and the levels of nitrogen oxides have been increasing in the city to dangerous levels, which is a clear sign of pollution from vehicles. Of these it is the diesel cars that are responsible for the pollution. Diesel emissions can trigger asthma and even cause lung cancer.

A survey by the Central Pollution Control Board and the All India Institute of Medical Sciences survey showed that a majority of people living in Delhi suffered from eye irritation, cough, sore throat, shortness of breath and poor lung functioning. One in 10 people have asthma in Delhi. Worse, the winter months bring respiratory attacks and wheezing to many non-asthmatics who are old, who smoke, have respiratory infections or chronic bronchitis.

Greenhouse Gas Emissions

India emits the fifth most carbon of any country in the world. At 253 million metric tons, only the U.S., China, Russia, and Japan surpassed its level of carbon emissions in 1998. Carbon emissions have grown nine-fold over the past forty years. In this Industrial Age, with the ever-expanding consumption of hydrocarbon fuels and the resultant increase in carbon dioxide emissions, that greenhouse gas concentrations have reached levels causing climate change. Going forward, carbon emissions are forecast to grow 3.2 per cent per annum until 2020. To put this in perspective, carbon emissions levels are estimated to increase by 3.9 per cent for China and by 1.3 per cent for the United States. India is a non-Annex I country under the United Nations Framework Convention on *Green house gases and climate Change* and as such, is not required to reduce its carbon emissions. An historical summary of carbon dioxide (CO_2) emissions from fossil fuel use in India is increasing rapidly and causes global warming.

All inhabitants of our planet have an equal right to the atmosphere, but the industrialized countries have greatly exceeded their fair, percapita share of the planet's atmospheric resources and have induced climate change. The most developed countries possess the capital, technological and human resources required for successful adaptation, while in the developing countries, a large proportion of the population is engaged in traditional farming, that is particularly vulnerable to the changes in temperature, rainfall and extreme weather events associated with climate change.

According to the UN Framework Convention on Climate Change and the Kyoto Protocol, the most industrialized countries are mainly responsible for causing climate change. Thus equity requires that they should sharply reduce their emissions in order to arrest further climate change and allow other countries access to their fair share of atmospheric resources in order to develop.

Pollution of Indian Seas

Two merchant vessels—MSC Chitra and Khalijia-III collided off the *Mumbai* coast on August 7, 2010 causing an oil spill. Several containers from one of the vessels fell into the sea. Nearly 100 containers that fell into the waters following the collision between two merchant vessels off the Mumbai coast are still missing and two of them are carrying hazardous chemicals reported on August 17, 2010. Describing the ship collision off the coast of Mumbai as a "freak accident", environment minister Jairam Ramesh said that India has never seen an oil spill like the one resulting from the incident.

A first-ever exercise on March 25, 2010, the country's 7500-km-long coastline will be surveyed to demarcate areas vulnerable to sea erosion, high tide and waves in order to help government take measures in protecting community living in such pockets. The Cabinet Committee of Economic Affairs (CCEA) approved a ₹ 1,156 crore Integrated Coastal Zone Management (ICZM) project which among other things cover coastline survey, capacity building of the people living near to coast, and demarcation of sensitive and hazardous zones.

The ship Platinum-II arrived in Indian waters on 8 October, 2009. The Ministry of Environment and Forests said it inspected Platinum-II and found the ship contained toxic material. The Platinum-II—formerly known as SS Oceanic or the SS Independence—was destined for the Alang ship-breaking yard. It is Asia's largest ship-breaking yard and known as the "graveyard of ships". It said many of the workers tested showed early signs of asbestosis—an incurable disease of the lungs. An unknown ship dumped tonnes of waste oil into the sea off Goa, creating tar balls that were heaping on Goa's famed beaches, September 1, 2010, officials said.

Indian Satellite to Monitor Green House Emission

A dedicated satellite would be launched with the support of Indian Space Research Organisation (ISRO) by 2012 to monitor Indias greenhouse gas emission, Union Minister for

Environment and Forests Jairam Ramesh said, "Currently, Japan and European countries have this satellite but by 2012 we will have a dedicated satellite that will monitor greenhouse gas emission across the country and globe." (March 13, 2010 at IIT-Powai).

"The objective is to study the impact of climate change, fallout of green house gas emissions on the environment by monitoring it through satellite technology," said fairam Ramesh. Another satellite for protection and development of the forest cover in India would be ready by 2013. "As the forests are getting depleted at a rapid pace elsewhere in the world, there seems to be a need for a satellite," Ramesh said.

Environmental Pollution and Chronic Diseases

In an Indo-US joint workshop, on September 05, 2008 at Chandigarh, Prof. S.K. Jindal said it has been globally recognised that environmental factors, have important links with infectious aswell as non-infectious diseases of both acute and chronic nature. "The WHO estimates that 24 per cent of global disease burden and 23 per cent of all deaths can be attributed to environmental factors. The burden is more on the developing than the developed countries." He said: "In developing countries, an estimated 42 per cent of acute lower respiratory infections are caused by environmental factors."

The major burden of these hazards is borne by the lungs. Bronchial *Asthma* and other allergies; chronic obstructive lung disease, respiratory infections including *tuberculosis* and occupational lung diseases are some of the common problems with a strong environmental risk which, account for a large disease burden all over the world, including in India. Extensive studies to gauge the effects of environmental factors on the human health needed.

According to *New England Journal of Medicine*, 2007, even a short exposure to traffic fumes can increase your chances of *Heart Disease,* including heart attack. People who exercise in areas where there is heavy traffic may be especially at risk, researchers say. Doctors at AIIMS, Delhi said on October 28, 2010 the incidence of rising strokes among the youngsters. "Lifestyle, environmental changes, growing pollution are the major causes for the increase," said Dr. Kameshwar Prasad, Professor, Neurology, AIIMS.

This gaseous air-pollutant along with other noxious gases emitted from the burning of fire-crackers on the eve of Diwali or Holi Festival aggravates the risk of triggering an attack in 30 mn asthmatics in India and also has the potential to cause new cases of asthma.

Poverty is the Biggest Polluter

During his meet with editors on July 01, 2011 Prime Minister Manmohan Singh remarked that "poverty is the biggest polluter" and India needs to achieve a balance between environment and development - industrialization. Indira Gandhi, the former Prime Minister announced at the United Nations first environmental Conference, in 1972 that "Poverty is the biggest polluter". Those sentiments were echoed by the Prime Minister, but Manmohan Singh have forgotten that Indira Gandhi created the country's environmental governance structure during her tenure as prime minister. It was Indira Gandhi's intervention that supported the call stop a hydro-electric project in Silent Valley, Kerala - saving an ecosystem rich in biodiversity. It was Indira Gandhi's concern that Mussorie, the queen of the hills, was being stripped naked by limestone mining that led the Environment Ministry to take action.

The poor live in the places polluted by the rich, they do not cause the pollution. And they live in polluted places because they are displaced from their homes in rural areas where they had lived sustainable for millennia. India's economy of sustenance is being uprooted by means of violence in order to enable POSCO to export our iron-ore and steel. In June, 2011 it was the women and children of Govindpur, Dinkia and Nuagaon in Odisha who laid down in front of the police in the scorching sun in an effort to stop the land grab. To farmers, tribles who form the bulk of protesters as *POSCO agitation against land acquisition* land is far more economically essential than a job of a petty unskilled worker in a factory.

The Most Polluted Places in India

Vapi in Gujarat and Sukinda in Odisha is among the world's top 10 most polluted places, according to the Blacksmith Institute, a New York-based non-profit group. Vapi returns to top, is again most polluted in country according to Central Pollution Control Board's interim report on May 21, 2012.

Vapi : Potentially affected people: 71,000 - Pollutants: Chemicals and heavy metals due to its Industrial estates.

Sukinda: Potentially affected people: 2,600,000. Pollutants: Hexavalent chromium due to its Chromite mines.

The Most Polluted Cities in India

As many as 51 Indian cities have extremely high air pollution, Patna, Lucknow, Raipur, Faridabad and Ahmedabad topping the list. An Environment and Forest Ministry report released on September 14, 2007 has identified 51 cities that do not meet the prescribed Respirable Suspended Particulate Matter (RSPM) levels, specified under the National Ambient Air Quality Standards (NAAQS). In 2005, an Environmental Sustainability Index (ESI) placed India at 101st position among 146 countries.

Taking a cue from the finding, the Central Pollution Control Board (CPCB) formulated NAAQS and checked the air quality, which led to the revelation about air quality in leading cities.

According to the report, Gobindgarh in Punjab is the most polluted city and Ludhiana, Raipur and Lucknow hold the next three positions. Faridabad on the outskirt of Delhi is the 10th most polluted city, followed by Agra, the city of Taj Mahal. Ahmedabad is placed 12th, Indore 16th, Delhi 22nd, Kolkata 25th, Mumbai 40th, Hyderabad 44th and Bangaluru stands at 46th in the list. The Odisha town of Angul, home to National Aluminium Company (NALCO), is the 50th polluted city of the country.

Emissions of Gaseous Pollutants: Satellite Data

Scientists and researchers from around the world gathered at ESRIN, ESA's Earth Observation Centre in Frascati, Italy, to discuss the contribution of satellite data in monitoring nitrogen dioxide in the atmosphere. Using nitrogen dioxide (NO_2) data acquired from 1996 to 2006 by the Global Ozone Monitoring Experiment (GOME) instrument aboard ESA's ERS-2 satellite. Nitrous oxide emissions over India is growing at an annual rate of 5.5 per cent/year. The location of emission hot spots correlates well with the location of mega thermal power plants, mega cities urban and industrial regions.

Emissions of gaseous pollutants have increased in India over the past two decades. According to Dr. Sachin Ghude of the Indian Institute of Tropical Meteorology (IITM), rapid industrialization, urbanization and traffic growth are most likely responsible for the increase. Because of varying consumption patterns and growth rates, the distribution of emissions vary widely across India.

Is Nuclear Energy a Solution of Global Warming?

India a country of 1.25 billion people currently gets only a fraction of its electricity from nuclear power. Now the US atomic trade pact with India and an atomic energy pact with France, India can fight global warming with clean nuclear energy. Nuclear energy has been recognized as a clean CO_2 to the atmosphere after its reaction that could damage our environment. It is also known that nuclear energy has reduced the amount of greenhouse gas emission, reducing emissions of CO_2 for about 500 million metric tonnes of carbon.

Indian Civil Liability for Nuclear Damage Bill, 2010 is meant to pave the way for India to sign International Atomic Energy Agency (IAEAs) Convention on Supplementary Compensation (CSC) for Nuclear Damage, 1997. The question that stares citizens in the face is: whether or not the proposed liability Bill and the pre-existing IAEAs compensation treaty in the supreme interest of present and future generation of Indians?

As on August 23, 2010 among the 18 amendments suggested to the Nuclear Liabilities Bill is one that leaves a window open for private operators of Nuclear plants. The standing committees had expressed its opinion against private operators.

India needs to learn appropriate lessons from the *worst nuclear accidents of Japan* and take additional safeguards, but the country cannot abandon its nuclear energy programme, said Minister for Environment and Forests, Jairam Ramesh on March 20, 2011.

Jaitapur, the site for India's largest nuclear power plant has taken again a violent turn on April 13, 2011 against the proposed nuclear power plant. Even as the world debates nuclear energy, here at ground zero in Jaitapur, the land has been taken over and the people have refused to accept any cheques of compensation from the State government.

Pollution due to Distilleries

The distillery sector is one of the seventeen categories of major polluting industries in India. These units generate large volume of dark brown coloured wastewater, which is known as 'spent wash' Spent wash contains high organic pollutants such as Total Dissolved Solids (TDS) - 85000 to 95,000 mg/l, Biochemical Oxygen Demand (BOD) - 45,000 to 60,000 mg/l and Chemical Oxygen Demarid (COD) 80,000 to 1,20,000 mg/l.

Thus, the distillery wastewater causes serious pollution problems in the recipient water bodies when discharged, resulting in depletion of dissolved oxygen in water and adverse affect on aquatic life, fish, phytoplankton etc. Also, it pollutes ground water and drinking water when discharged on land. Application of distillery wastewater for irrigation of crops causes soil pollution *i.e.,* salinity.

The Government has notified environmental standards for the distillery sector under the Environment (Protection) Act, 1986. The Government is also encouraging the distilleries to achieve zero discharge of effluent. This information was given by Shri Jairam Ramesh in Lok Sabha on August 4, 2010.

Suggestions/Conclusions

Projects to Save Agra Monuments back on Trac

The growing threat from pollution to India's prized monuments, including the Taj Mahal, has prompted the authorities to speed up action on March 22, 2011. The project aims to insulate the world heritage monuments, including Fatehpur Sikri, Agra Fort and the Taj Mahal. A set of eight schemes to control pollution and save these monuments has been submitted for clearance from the state government before being presented to the Planning Commission to include them in the 12th Five-year Plan (2012-2017).

World Bank Cooperation on India's Green Agenda

India and the World Bank agreed on January 13, 2011 to further strengthen their partnership to advance India's green-growth agenda. The Bank will now support to strengthen Indian capacity of Central Pollution Controls Board, State Pollution Control Boards and biodiversity conservation in addition to other various projects for which financial support have already been given.

India to Build Advanced Coal-fired Power Plant

Indian scientists aim to built an advanced ultra-super critical coal-fired power plant in the next six years. Once realised, the plant is expected to put India in a very select group of nations having the technology which would reduce the amount of pollution when compared with the current thermal power plants.

Green Court Launched

India launched a "green" court on October 19, 2010 to make polluters pay damages as it steps up its policing of the country's environmental laws. Environment Minister Jairam Ramesh said India was only the third country in the world after Australia and New Zealand to set up such a tribunal. "This is the first body of its kind (in India) to apply the polluter pays principle and the principle of sustainable development," Ramesh told reporters in New Delhi.

National Action Plan on Climate Change

The Centre has made a provision of ₹ 25,000 crore to mitigate the effects of climate change, a serious problem that India will face in the coming decades, Minister of State for Environment and Forests Jairam Ramesh told the Rajya Sabha on August 21, 2010. Besides, the Finance Ministry has also sanctioned ₹ 5,000 crore as recommended by the 13th Finance Commission to tackle this serious problem," Mr. Ramesh said About 220 scientists from 120 research institutions were working on assessing the impact of climate change on agriculture, water, health and forests.

National Clean Energy Fund (NCEF) - for funding research and innovative projects in clean energy technology. Allocation for National Ganga River Basin Authority has been doubled in 2010-11 to ₹ 500 crore. The "Mission Clean Ganga 2020" under the National Ganga River Basin Authority (NGRBA) with the objective that no untreated municipal sewage or industrial influent will be discharged into the National river has already been initiated.

11

Water Pollution
Causes, Measurement and its Control

P. Divakara Rao
Lecturer in Commerce, Govt. Degree College, Tuni, East Godavari District, Andhra Pradesh

Introduction

Water pollution is the contamination of water bodies (*e.g.*, lakes, rivers, oceans, aquifers and groundwater). Water pollution occurs when pollutants are discharged directly or indirectly into water bodies without adequate treatment to remove harmful compounds.

Millions Depend on the Polluted Ganges River

Raw Sewage and Industrial Waste in the River

Water pollution affects plants and organisms living in these bodies of water. In almost all cases the effect is damaging not only to individual species and populations, but also to the natural biological communities.

Water pollution is a major global problem which requires ongoing evaluation and revision of water resource policy at all levels (international down to individual aquifers and wells). It has been suggested that it is the leading worldwide cause of deaths and diseases and that it accounts for the deaths of more than 14,000 people daily. An estimated 700 million Indians have no access to a proper toilet and 1,000 Indian children die of diarrhoeal sickness every day. Some 90 per cent of China's cities suffer from some degree of water pollution and nearly 500 million people lack access to safe drinking water. In addition to the acute problems of water pollution in developing countries, developed countries continue to struggle with pollution problems as well. In the most recent national report on water quality in the United States, 45 per cent of assessed stream miles, 47 per cent of assessed lake acres and 32 per cent of assessed bays and estuarine square miles were classified as polluted.

Water is typically referred to as polluted when it is impaired by anthropogenic contaminants and either does not support a human use, such as drinking water and/or undergoes a marked shift in its ability to support its constituent biotic communities, such as fish. Natural phenomena such as volcanoes, algae blooms, storms and earthquakes also cause major changes in water quality and the ecological status of water.

Categories

Surface water and groundwater have often been studied and managed as separate resources, although they are interrelated. Surface water seeps through the soil and becomes groundwater. Conversely, groundwater can also feed surface water sources. Sources of surface water pollution are generally grouped into two categories based on their origin.

Point sources

Point source water pollution refers to contaminants that enter a waterway from a single, identifiable source, such as a pipe or ditch. Examples of sources in this category include discharges from a sewage treatment plant, a factory, or a city storm drain. The U.S. Clean Water Act (CWA) defines point source for regulatory enforcement purposes. The CWA definition of point source was amended in 1987 to include municipal storm sewer systems, as well as industrial storm water, such as from construction sites.

Point source pollution - Shipyard - Rio de Janeiro.

Non-point Sources

Non-point source pollution refers to diffuse contamination that does not originate from a single discrete source. NFS pollution is often the cumulative effect of small amounts of contaminants gathered from a large area. A common example is the leaching out of nitrogen compounds from fertilized agricultural lands. Nutrient runoff in storm water from "sheet flow" over an agricultural field or a forest are also cited as examples of NFS pollution.

Contaminated storm water washed off of parking lots, roads and highways, called urban runoff, is sometimes included under the category of NFS pollution. However, this runoff is typically channeled into storm drain systems and discharged through pipes to local surface waters and is a point source.

Groundwater Pollution

Groundwater Pollution and Hydrogeology

Interactions between groundwater and surface water are complex. Consequently, groundwater pollution, sometimes referred to as **groundwater contamination,** is not as easily classified as surface water pollution. By its very nature, groundwater aquifers are susceptible to contamination from sources that may not directly affect surface water bodies, and the distinction of point vs. non-point source may be irrelevant. A spill or ongoing releases of chemical or radionuclide contaminants into soil (located away from a surface water body) may not create point source or non-point source pollution, but can contaminate the aquifer below, defined as a toxin plume. The movement of the plume, called a plume front, may be analyzed through a hydrological transport model or groundwater model. Analysis of groundwater contamination may focus on the soil characteristics and site geology, hydrogeology, hydrology, and the nature of the contaminants.

Causes

The specific contaminants leading to pollution in water include a wide spectrum of chemicals, pathogens and physical or sensory changes such as elevated temperature and discolaration. While many of the chemicals and substances that are regulated may be naturally occurring (calcium, sodium, iron, manganese, etc.) the concentration is often the key in determining what is a natural component of water and what is a contaminant. High concentrations of naturally occurring substances can have negative impacts on aquatic flora and fauna.

Oxygen-depleting substances may be natural materials, such as plant matter (*e.g.*, leaves and grass) as well as man-made chemicals. Other natural and anthropogenic substances may cause turbidity (cloudiness) which blocks light and disrupts plant growth, and clogs the gills of some fish species.

Many of the chemical substances are toxic. Pathogens can produce waterborne diseases in either human or animal hosts. Alteration of water's physical chemistry includes acidity (change in pH), electrical conductivity, temperature, and eutrophication. Eutrophication is an increase in the concentration of chemical nutrients in an ecosystem to an extent that increases in the primary productivity of the ecosystem. Depending on the degree of eutrophication, subsequent negative environmental effects such as anoxia (oxygen depletion) and severe reductions in water quality may occur, affecting fish and other animal populations.

Pathogens

Coliform bacteria are a commonly used bacterial indicator of water pollution, although not an actual cause of disease. Other microorganisms sometimes found in surface waters which have caused human health problems include:

- *Burkholderia pseudomallei*
- *Cryptosporidium parvum*
- *Giardia lamblia*
- *Salmonella*
- *Novovirus and other viruses*
- *Parasitic worms (helrninths).*

High levels of pathogens may result from inadequately treated sewage discharges. This can be caused by a sewage plant designed with less than secondary treatment (more typical in less-developed countries). In developed countries, older cities with aging infrastructure may have leaky sewage collection systems (pipes, pumps, valves), which can cause sanitary sewer overflows. Some cities also have combined sewers, which may discharge untreated sewage during rain storms.

Pathogen discharges may also be caused by poorly managed livestock operations.

Chemical and Other Contaminants

Contaminants may include organic and inorganic substances.

Organic water pollutants include:

- Detergents
- Disinfection by-products found in chemically disinfected drinking water, such as chloroform
- Food processing waste, which can include oxygen-demanding substances, fats and grease
- Insecticides and herbicides, a huge range of organohalides and other chemical compounds
- Petroleum hydrocarbons, including fuels (gasoline, diesel fuel, jet fuels, and ftiel oil) and lubricants (motor oil), and fuel combustion byproducts, from stormwater runoff
- Tree and bush debris from logging operations
- Volatile organic compounds (VOCs), such as industrial solvents, from improper storage.
- Chlorinated solvents, which are dense non-aqueous phase liquids (DNAPLs), may fall to the bottom of reservoirs, since they don't mix well with water and are denser.
  - Polychlorinated biphenyl (PCBs)
  - Trichloroethylene
- Perchlorate.

Various chemical compounds found in personal hygiene and cosmetic products.

Macroscopic Pollution

Inorganic water pollutants include:

- Acidity caused by industrial discharges (especially sulfur dioxide from power plants).
- Ammonia from food processing waste.
- Chemical waste as industrial by products.
- Fertilizers containing nutrients—nitrates and phosphates—which are found in stormwater runoff from agriculture, as well as commercial and residential use.
- Heavy metals from motor vehicles (via urban stormwater runoff) and acid mine drainage.
- Silt (sediment) in runoff from construction sites, logging, slash and burn practices or land clearing sites.

Macroscopic pollution—large visible items polluting the water—may be termed "floatables" in an urban stormwater context, or marine debris when found on the open seas, and can include such items as:

- Trash or garbage (*e.g.*, paper, plastic, or food waste) discarded by people on the ground, along with accidental or intentional dumping of rubbish, that are washed by rainfall into storm drains and eventually discharged into surface waters.

- Nurdles, small ubiquitous waterborne plastic pellets
- Shipwrecks, large derelict ships.

Thermal Pollution

Thermal pollution is the rise or fall in the temperature of a natural body of water caused by human influence. Thermal pollution, unlike chemical pollution, results in a change in the physical properties of water. A common cause of thermal pollution is the use of water as a coolant by power plants and industrial manufacturers. Elevated water temperatures decreases oxygen levels, which can kill fish, and can alter food chain composition, reduce species biodiversity, and foster invasion by new thermophilic species. Urban runoff may also elevate temperature in surface waters.

Thermal pollution can also be caused by the release of very cold water from the base of reservoirs into warmer rivers.

Transport and Chemical Reactions of Water Pollutants

Most water pollutants are eventually carried by rivers into the oceans. In some areas of the world the influence can be traced hundred miles from the mouth by studies using hydrology transport models. Advanced computer models such as SWMM or the DSSAM Model have been used in many locations worldwide to examine the fate of pollutants in aquatic systems. Indicator filter feeding species such as copepods have also been used to study pollutant fates in the New York Bight, for example. The highest toxin loads are not directly at the mouth of the Hudson River, but 100 kilometers south, since several days are required for incorporation into planktonic tissue. The Hudson discharge flows south along the coast due to coriolis force. Further south then are areas of oxygen depletion, caused by chemicals using up oxygen and by algae blooms, caused by excess nutrients from algal cell death and decomposition. Fish and shellfish kills have been reported, because toxins climb the food chain after small fish consume copepods, then large fish eat smaller fish, etc. Each successive step up the food chain causes a stepwise concentration of pollutants such as heavy metals (*e.g.*, mercury) and persistent organic pollutants such as DDT.

This is known as biomagnification, which is occasionally used interchangeably with bio accumulation.

Large gyres (vortexes) in the oceans trap floating plastic debris. The North Pacific Gyre for example has collected the so-called "Great Pacific Garbage Patch" that is now estimated at 100 times the size of Texas. Many of these long-lasting pieces wind up in the stomachs of marine birds and animals. This results in obstruction of digestive pathways which leads to reduced appetite or even starvation.

Many chemicals undergo reactive decay or chemically change especially over long periods of time in groundwater reservoirs. A noteworthy class of such chemicals is the chlorinated hydrocarbons such as trichloroethylene (used in industrial metal degreasing and electronics manufacturing) and tetrachloroethylene used in the dry cleaning industry (note latest advances in liquid carbon dioxide in dry cleaning that avoids all use of chemicals). Both of these chemicals, which are carcinogens themselves, undergo partial decomposition reactions, leading to new hazardous chemicals (including dichloroethylene and vinyl chloride).

Groundwater pollution is much more difficult to abate than surface pollution because groundwater can move great distances through unseen aquifers. Non-porous aquifers such as clays partially purify water of bacteria by simple filtration (adsorption and absorption), dilution and, in some cases, chemical reactions and biological activity: however, in some cases, the pollutants merely transform to soil contaminants. Groundwater that moves through cracks and caverns is not filtered and can be transported as easily as surface water. In fact, this can be aggravated by the human tendency to use natural sinkholes as dumps in areas of Karst topography.

There are a variety of secondary effects stemming not from the original pollutant, but a derivative condition. An example is silt-bearing surface runoff, which can inhibit the penetration of sunlight through the water column, hampering photosynthesis in aquatic plants.

Measurement

Water pollution may be analyzed through several broad categories of methods: physical, chemical and biological. Most involve collection of samples, followed by specialized analytical tests. Some methods may be conducted *in situ,* without sampling, such as temperature. Government agencies and research organizations have published standardized, validated analytical test methods to facilitate the comparability of results from disparate testing events.'

Sampling

Sampling of water for physical or chemical testing can be done by several methods, depending on the accuracy needed and the characteristics of the contaminant. Many contamination events are sharply restricted in time, most commonly in association with rain events. For this reason "grab" samples are often inadequate for fully quantifying contaminant levels. Scientists gathering this type of data often employ auto-sampler devices that pump increments of water at either time or discharge intervals.

Sampling for biological testing involves collection of plants and/or animals from the surface water body. Depending on the type of assessment, the organisms may be identified for biosurveys (population counts) and returned to the water body, or they may be dissected for bio ass ays to determine toxicity.

Physical Testing

Common physical tests of water include temperature, solids concentrations (*e.g.,* total suspended solids (TSS)) and turbidity.

Chemical Testing

Water samples may be examined using the principles of analytical chemistry. Many published test methods are available for both organic and inorganic compounds. Frequently used methods include pH, biochemical oxygen demand (BOD), chemical oxygen demand (COD), nutrients (nitrate and phosphorus compounds), metals (including copper, zinc, cadmium, lead and mercury), oil and grease, total petroleum hydrocarbons (TPH) and pesticides.

Control of Pollution

Domestic Sewage

Domestic sewage is 99.9 per cent pure water, while the other 0.1 percent are pollutants. Although found in low concentrations, these pollutants pose risk on a large scale. In urban areas, domestic sewage is typically treated by centralized sewage treatment plants. In the U.S., most of these plants are operated by local government agencies, frequently referred to as publicly owned treatment works (POTW). Municipal treatment plants are designed to control conventional pollutants: BOD and suspended solids. Well-designed and operated systems (*i.e.*, secondary treatment or better) can remove 90 per cent or more of these pollutants. Some plants have additional sub-systems to treat nutrients and pathogens. Most municipal plants are not designed to treat toxic pollutants found in industrial wastewater.

Cities with sanitary sewer overflows or combined sewer overflows employ one or more engineering approaches to reduce discharges of untreated sewage, including:

- utilizing a green infrastructure approach to improve stormwater management capacity throughout the system, and reduce the hydraulic overloading of the treatment plant.
- repair and replacement of leaking and malfunctioning equipment.
- increasing overall hydraulic capacity of the sewage collection system (often a very expensive option).

A household or business not served by a municipal treatment plant may have an individual septic tank, which treats the wastewater on site and discharges into the soil. Alternatively, domestic wastewater may be sent to a nearby privately owned treatment system (*e.g.*, in a rural community).

Industrial Wastewater

Some industrial facilities generate ordinary domestic sewage that can be treated by municipal facilities. Industries that generate wastewater with high concentrations of conventional pollutants (*e.g.*, oil and grease), toxic pollutants (*e.g.*, heavy metals, volatile organic compounds) or other nonconventional pollutants such as ammonia, need specialized treatment systems. Some of these facilities can install a pre-treatment system to remove the toxic components, and then send the partially treated wastewater to the municipal system. Industries generating large volumes of wastewater typically operate their own complete on-site treatment systems.

Some industries have been successful at redesigning their manufacturing processes to reduce or eliminate pollutants, through a process called pollution prevention.

Heated water generated by power plants or manufacturing plants may be controlled with:

- cooling ponds, man-made bodies of water designed for cooling by evaporation, convection and radiation.
- cooling towers, which transfer waste heat to the atmosphere through evaporation and/or heat transfer.
- cogeneration, a process where waste heat is recycled for domestic and/or industrial heating purposes.

Agricultural Wastewater

Non-Point Source Controls

Sediment (loose soil) washed off fields is the largest source of agricultural pollution in the United States. Farmers may utilize erosion controls to reduce runoff flows and retain soil on their fields. Common techniques include contour plowing, crop mulching, crop rotation, planting perennial crops and installing riparian buffers.

Nutrients (nitrogen and phosphorus) are typically applied to farmland as commercial fertilizer; animal manure; or spraying of municipal or industrial wastewater (effluent) or sludge. Nutrients may also enter runoff from crop residues, irrigation water, wildlife and atmospheric deposition. Farmers can develop and implement nutrient management plans to reduce excess application of nutrients.

To minimize pesticide impacts, farmers may use Integrated Pest Management (IPM) techniques (which can include biological pest control) to maintain control over pests, reduce reliance on chemical pesticides, and protect water quality.

Point Source Wastewater Treatment

Farms with large livestock and poultry operations, such as factory farms, are called *concentrated animal feeding operations orfeedlots* in the US and are being subject to increasing government regulation. Animal slurries are usually treated by containment in anaerobic lagoons before disposal by spray or trickle application to grassland. Constructed wetlands are sometimes used to facilitate treatment of animal wastes. Some animal slurries are treated by mixing with straw and composted at high temperature to produce a bacteriologically sterile and friable manure for soil improvement.

Construction Site Stormwater

Sediment from construction sites is managed by installation of:

- erosion controls, such as mulching and hydroseeding, and
- sediment controls, such as sediment basins and silt fences.

Discharge of toxic chemicals such as motor fuels and concrete washout is prevented by use of:

- spill prevention and control plans, and

- specially designed containers (*e.g.*, for concrete washout) and structures such as overflow controls and diversion berms.

Urban Runoff (Stormwater)

Effective control of urban runoff involves reducing the velocity and flow of stormwater, as well as reducing pollutant discharges. Local governments use a variety of stormwater management techniques to reduce the effects of urban runoff. These techniques, called best management practices (BMPs) in the U.S., may focus on water quantity control, while others focus on improving water quality and some perform both functions.

Conclusion

Pollution prevention practices include low-impact development techniques, installation of green roofs and improved chemical handling (*e.g.*, management of motor fuels & oil, fertilizers and pesticides). Runoff mitigation systems include infiltration basins, bioretention systems, constructed wetlands, retention basins and similar devices.

Thermal pollution from runoff can be controlled by stormwater management facilities that absorb the runoff or direct it into groundwater, such as bioretention systems and infiltration basins. Retention basins tend to be less effective at reducing temperature, as the water may be heated by the sun before being discharged to a receiving stream.

REFERENCES

1. "A special report on India: Creaking, Groaning: Infrastructure is India's biggest handicap". *The Economist*. December 11, 2008.
2. "As China Roars, Pollution Reaches Deadly Extremes". *The New York Times*. August 26, 2007.
3. "China says water pollution so severe that cities could lack safe supplies". Chinadaily.com.cn. June 7, 2005.
4. Clean Water Act, section 502(14), 33 U.S.C. § 1362(14)

5. CWA section 402(p), 33 U.S.C. § 1342(p).
6. EPA. "Illness Related to Sewage in Water." Accessed February 20, 2009.
7. EPA. "Report to Congress: Impacts and Control of CSOs and SSOs." August 2004. Document No. EPA-833-R-04-001.
8. Hogan, C. Michael (2010). "Water pollution." *Encyclopedia of Earth.* Topic ed. Mark McGinley; ed. in chief C. Cleveland. National Council on Science and the Environment, Washington, DC.
9. Pink, Daniel H. (April 19, 2006). "Investing in Tomorrow's Liquid Gold". Yahoo.
10. Schueler, Thomas R. "Microbes and Urban Watersheds: Concentrations, Sources, & Pathways." Reprinted in *The Practice of Watershed Protection.* 2000. Center for Watershed Protection. Ellicott City, MD.
11. United States Environmental Protection Agency (EPA). Washington, DC. "The National Water Quality Inventory: Report to Congress for the 2002 Reporting Cycle—A Profile." October 2007. *Fact Sheet No. EPA 841-F-07-003.*
12. United States Geological Survey (USGS), Denver, CO (1998). "Ground Water and Surface Water: A Single Resource." Circular 1139.
13. USGS. Reston, VA. "A Primer on Water Quality." FS-027-01. March 2001.
14. West, Larry (March 26, 2006). "World Water Day: A Billion People Worldwide Lack Safe Drinking Water". About.
15. Water Quality from Agricultural Runoff." Fact Sheet No. EPA-841-F-05-001. March 2005.

Carbon Trading for a Greater Planet

Madasu Veerender
Lecturer in Commerce
Girraj Govt. College (A),
Nizamabad

Introduction

The burning of fossil fuels is a major source of greenhouse gas emissions, especially for power, cement, steel, textile, fertilizer and many other industries which rely on fossil fuels (coal, electricity derived from coal, natural gas and oil). The major greenhouse gases emitted by these industries are carbon dioxide, methane, nitrous oxide, hydro flurocarbons (HFCs), etc., all of which increase the atmosphere's ability to trap infrared energy and thus affect the climate.

The past few decades have witnessed a growing awareness of not only the severity but also the diversity of environmental problems. Global environmental concerns such as acid rain, ozone depletion, climate change, habitat, bio-diversity loss etc. have triggered international environmental actions. Regional and local problems – such as depletion of renewable resources, flood and drought, deterioration of air and water quality etc. – have also been the subject of public debate and governmental action. An increasing number of environmental problems compete for places on political agenda of the nations, for the attention of regulatory agencies and international goernment bodies and for the limited resources available for environmental management.

Environment was higher to a subject for academicians and scientists but lately the world community has realized that without protecting the Environment, we shall be marching to manmade destruction. This realisation has made Environment not only a global, national or state subject but also a concern for one and all. It has entered the Board rooms factories and business premises with economic, social and legal consequences. Business cannot be established or run or shifted or even abandoned without environmental clearances. Companies with their eyes on growth and market share are already focusing on greening themselves. The increasing concern for Environment, both in public and industry, is compelling management to build synergy, between their Economic and Environmental Policies because sound Environmental Management provides the company a competitive advantage in addition to fulfilling the corporate social responsibility and adding value to the business. While majority of the industries is stuck up with compliance of Environmental laws, some have moved beyond legislation. They have also taken to broader environmental issues like acid rain, ozone depletion, global wanning etc. TISCO, the most cost effective Steel Company has reported its environmental performance in GRI format which has been duly verified by Pricewaterhouse Coopers. The company has exceeded regulatory compliance standards. It has achieved a reduction in Greenhouse Gas (GHG) emissions by 9.0 per cent (against a target of 5%) , specific energy consumption by 1.8 per cent (against a target of 4%), raw material consumption by 10.8 per cent (against a target of 5%), water consumption by 10.2 per cent (against a target of 5%) and, has increased waste reuse and recycling from 70.2 per cent to 72.6 per cent (against a target of 72%) during the year. The Company has also undertaken a Clean Development Mechanism (CDM) project.

Carbon trading is the name given to the exchange of emission permits. This transition may take place within the economy or may take the form of international transition. There are two types of carbon trading namely emission trading and offset trading.

Carbon trading is a new mechanism designed to allow firms that fail to meet the emission standards set by the 1997 Kyoto Protocol, to buy credits from other firms that meet their target The Kyoto Protocol was initiated by the United Nations Framework Convention on Climate Change and ratified by 181 countries and the European Union as a whole, individual entity in 1997 and was put into effect in 2005. The Kyoto Protocol also envisaged carbon credit trade between countries with carbon sinks *i.e.*, planted forests and other that produce higher level of pollution. Each Annex-I has been assigned fixed amount in Kyoto Protocol agreement. This amount is actually the amount of emission which is to be reduced by the concerned country.

Such fixed amount implies that the country is permitted to emit the remaining amount. This emission allowance is actually one kind of carbon credit. The total amount of allowance is then subdivided into certain units. The units are expressed in tenns of carbon equivalent. Each unit gives the owner the right to emit one metric ton of carbon dioxide or other equivalent green house gases.

Another variant of carbon credit is to be earned by a country by investing some amount in such project, known as carbon projects which will emit lesser amount of green house gas in the atmosphere. The exchange of first variant of carbon credit is known as emission trading or cap- and trade whereas exchange of second variant of carbon credit is termed as offset trading. It is one of the ways through which countries can meet their obligation under the Kyoto Protocol.

The world's only mandatory carbon trading programme is the European Union. Emissions Trading Scheme, created in conjunction with the Kyoto Protocol, it took effect in 2005, and it caps the amount of large installations, such as power plants and factories in the European Union countries.

Global carbon trading has gained momentum. The world watch Institute drawing from various studies, places the value of the trade at about 60 billion dollars in 2007. Asian countries are biggest sellers and western countries are biggest buyers.

India is considered a major supplier of certified emission reductions because of the largest number of projects registered with the clean development mechanism. More than a hundred projects from India have been issued CERs for a total of 25 million. India has also taken a highly proactive approach to CDM from the very beginning and playing a major role in the design of the mechanism and its modalities. India also ranks first in registration of CDM projects followed by Brazil, Mexico and China. About 740 million CERs are expected from registered projects till 2012. The large scale CDM development in India is due to the fact that the country is endowed with skilled human resources to handle this task.

The growing Indian economy and its diverse sectors offer huge potential for emission reduction. Most of the CDM projects in renewable energy sector. The energy efficiency and industrial process were other sector. However, the average six of the CDM projects from India is 3000-5000 CERs per annum per project. India has also offered the largest number of CDM projects so far to the CDM Executive Board.

Carbon dioxide, the most important greenhouse gas produced by combustion of fuels, has become a cause of global panic as its concentration in the Earth's atmosphere has been rising alarmingly.

This devil, however, is now turning into a product that helps people, countries, consultants, traders, corporations and even farmers earn billions of rupees. This was an unimaginable trading opportunity not more than a decade ago.

Carbon credits are a part of international emission trading norms. They incentivise companies or countries that emit less carbon. The total annual emissions are capped and the market allocates a monetary value to any shortfall through trading. Businesses can exchange, buy or sell carbon credits in international markets at the prevailing market price.

India and China are likely to emerge as the biggest sellers and Europe is going to be the biggest buyers of carbon credits.

Carbon Credit

A carbon credit is a generic term for any tradable certificate or permit representing the right to emit one tone of carbon dioxide or the mass of another greenhouse gas with a carbon dioxide equivalent (tCC_2e) to one tonne of carbon dioxide. Carbon credits create a market for reducing greenhouse emissions by giving a monetary value to the cost of polluting the air. Emissions become an internal cost of doing business and are visible on the balance sheet alongside raw materials and other assets and liabilities.

As nations have progressed we have been emitting carbon, or gases which result in warming of the globe. Some decades ago a debate started on how to reduce the emission of harmful gases that contributes to the greenhouse effect that causes global wanning. So, countries came together and signed an agreement named the Kyoto Protocol.

The Kyoto Protocol has created a mechanism under which countries that have been emitting more carbon and other gases (greenhouse gases include ozone, carbon dioxide, methane, nitrous oxide and even water vapour) have voluntarily decided that they will bring down the level of carbon they are emitting to the levels of early 1990s.

Developed countries, mostly European, had said that they will bring down the level in the period from 2008 to 2012. In 2008, these developed countries have decided on different norms to bring down the level of emission fixed for their companies and factories.

A company has two ways to reduce emissions. One, it can reduce the GHG (greenhouse gases) by adopting new technology or improving upon the existing technology to attain the new norms for emission of gases. Or it can tie up with developing nations and help them set up new technology that is eco-friendly, thereby helping developing country or its companies 'earn' credits.

The ones who are selling are companies that use clean technology and those buying are the world's polluters. In future, the menace of global warming can be effectively handled by this system.

India, China and some other Asian countries have the advantage because they are developing countries. Any company, factories or farm owner in India can get linked to United Nations Framework Convention on Climate Change (UNFCCC) and know the 'standard' level of carbon emission allowed for its outfit or activity. The extent to which I am emitting less carbon (as per standard fixed by UNFCCC) we get credited in a developing country. This is called carbon credit. Every transaction has to be ratified by UNFCCC, for European Union, in addition to this European Commision's ratification is necessary.

These credits are bought over by the companies of developed countries—mostly Europeans—because the United States has not signed the Kyoto Protocol.

Additionality and Its Importance

It is also important for any carbon credit (offset) to prove a concept called additionality. The concept of additionality addresses the question of whether the project would have happened anyway, even in the absence of revenue from carbon credits. Only carbon credits from projects that are "additional to" the business-as-usual scenario represent a net environmental benefit. Carbon projects that yield strong financial returns even in the absence of revenue from carbon credits; or that are compelled by regulations; or that represent common practice in an industry are usually not considered additional, although a full determination of additionality requires specialist review. It is generally agreed that voluntary carbon offset projects must also prove additionality in order to ensure the legitimacy of the environmental stewardship claims resulting from the retirement of the carbon credit (offset).

In Real Life how it helps a Common Man

Assume that British Petroleum is running a plant in the United Kingdom. Say, that it is emitting more gases than the accepted norms of the UNFCCC. It can tie up with its own subsidiary in, say, India or China under the Clean Development Mechanism. It can buy the 'carbon credit' by making Indian or Chinese plant more eco-savvy with the help of technology transfer. It can tie up with any other company like Indian Oil, or anybody else, in the open market.

In December 2008, an audit will be done of their efforts to reduce gases and their actual level of emission. China and India are ensuring that new technologies for energy savings are adopted so that they become entitled for more carbon credits. They are selling their credits to their counterparts in Europe. This is how a market for carbon credit is created.

Clean Development Mechanism

Under the CDM you can cut the deal for carbon credit. Under the UNFCCC, charter any company from the developed world can tie up with a company in the developing country that is a signatory to the Kyoto Protocol. These companies in developing countries must adopt newer technologies, emitting lesser gases, and save energy.

Only a portion of the total earnings of carbon credits of the company can be transferred to the company of the developed countries under CDM. There is a fixed quota on buying of credit by companies in Europe.

MCX Trading in Carbon Credits

This entire process was not understood well by many. Those who knew about the possibility of earning profits, adopted new technologies, saved credits and sold it to improve their bottomline.

Many companies did not apply to get credit even though they had new technologies. Some companies used management consultancies to make their plan greener to emit less GHG. These management consultancies then scouted for buyers to sell carbon credits. It was a bilateral deal.

However, the price to sell carbon credits was not available on a public platform. The price range people were getting used to be about Euro 15 or maybe less per tonne of carbon. Today, one tonne of carbon credit fetches around Euro 22. It is traded on the European Climate Exchange. Therefore, you emit one tonne less and you get Euro 22. Emit less and increase/add to your profit.

The Multi-Commodity Exchange (MCX) of India may soon become the third exchange in the world to trade in carbon credits. The MCX decided to trade carbon credits in futures trading. Let people judge if they want to hold on to their accumulated carbon credits or sell them now. MCX has become first exchange in Asia to trade carbon credits.

There are parameters set and detailed audit is done before you get the entitlement to sell the credit. In India, already 300 to 400 companies have carbon credits after meeting UNFCCC norms. Till MCX came along, these companies were not getting best-suited price. Some were getting Euro 15 and some were getting Euro 18 through bilateral agreements. When the contract expires in December, it is expected that prices will be firm up then.

On MCX has already had power, energy and metal companies who are trading. These companies are high-energy consuming companies. They need better technology to emit less carbon.

Involvement of Small Investor

These carbon credits are with the large manufacturing companies who are adopting UNFCCC norms. Retail investors can come in the market and buy the contract if they think the market of carbon is going to firm up. Like any other asset they can buy these too. It is kept in the form of an electronic certificate.

MCX would keeping the registry and the ownership will travel from the original owner to the next buyer. In the short-term, large investors are likely to come and later we expect banks to get into the market too. This business is a function of money, and someone will have to hold on to these big transactions to sell at the appropriate time.

Polluters in Europe to Buy Carbon Credit and Get Away with it

It is incorrect to say that because under UNFCCC the polluters cannot buy 100 per cent of the carbon credits they are required to reduce. Say, out of 100 per cent they have to induce 75 per cent locally by various means in their own country. They can buy only 25 per cent of carbon credits from developing countries.

Role of India in Carbon Trading

India is emerging as a serious player in the global carbon credits market. This has prompted originator, developer and trader of carbon credits, to set up office in India. Carbon credit is very emerging domain now a day's especially in India but very few corporate are aware of this emerging segment. At present it is quite essential to create awareness about this business segment. As, India's GHG emission is below. The target and so, it is entitled to sell surplus credits to developed countries. India is considered to claim about 31 per cent of the total world carbon trade, which can give $25bn by 2010. This is what makes trading in carbon credits such a great business opportunity. Foreign companies which cannot fulfil the norms can buy the surplus credit from companies in other countries. Many Indian companies have been re-rated on the stock markets on the basis of the bonanza that will accrue to them when carbon trading kicks off. SRF Ltd and Shell frading International have entered into sale and purchase Credit Emission Reduction. Suzlon Energy and Shriram EPC have business in wind energy which is eligible for carbon credit benefits. Shree Renuka Sugars is also expected to benefit from carbon credits. Gujarat Flourochemicals was among the early companies to register for Clean Development Mechanism (COM) project. India has emerged as the dark horse in this race as more than 200 Indian entities have applied for registering their CDM Project for availing carbon credits. The 800 million farming community in India has also a unique opportunity where they can sell Carbon Credits to developed nations. The India's Delhi Metro Rail Corporation (DMRC) has become the first rail project in the world to earn carbon credits because of using regenerative braking system in its rolling stock. DMRC has earned the carbon credits by using regenerative braking system in its trains that reduces 30 per cent electricity consumption it is believed that it is not the penalty awarded to erring companies, but the rewards and recognition given to green firms is what makes this system so popular and exclusive.

This means that companies with limited emissions will devise strategies to further reduce emissions so that they can sell more carbon credits in the international market and thereby increase their profits. Thus, the system keeps on de-polluting the environment increasingly. Last year global carbon credit trading was estimated at $5 billion, with India's contribution at around $1 billion. India is one of the countries that have 'credits' for emitting less carbon. India and China have surplus credit to offer to countries that have a deficit.

India has generated some 30 million carbon credits and has roughly another 140 million to push into the world market. Waste disposal units, plantation companies, chemical plants and municipal corporations can sell the carbon credits and make money.

Carbon Trading vs. Carbon Taxation

Carbon credits and carbon taxes each have their advantages and disadvantages. Credits were chosen by the signatories to the Kyoto Protocol as an alternative to carbon taxes. A criticism of tax-raising schemes is that they are frequently not hypothecated, and so some or all of the taxation raised by a government would be applied based on what the particular nation's government deems most fitting. However, some would argue that carbon trading is based around creating a lucrative artificial market, and, handled by free market enterprises as it is, carbon trading is not necessarily a focused or easily regulated solution.

By treating emissions as a market commodity some proponents insist it becomes easier for businesses to understand and manage their activities, while economists and traders can attempt to predict future pricing using market theories. Thus the main advantages of a traceable carbon credit over a carbon tax are argued to be:

- The price may be more likely to be perceived as fair by those paying it. Investors in credits may have more control over their own costs.
- The flexible mechanisms of the Kyoto Protocol help to ensure that all investment goes into genuine sustainable carbon reduction schemes through an internationally agreed validation process.
- Some proponents state that if correctly implemented a target level of emission reductions may somehow be achieved with more certainty, while under a tax the actual emissions might vary over time.
- It may provide a framework for rewarding people or companies who plant trees or otherwise meet standards exclusively recognized as "green".

The advantages of a carbon tax are argued to be:

- Possibly less complex, expensive, and time-consuming to implement. This advantage is especially great when applied to markets like gasoline or home heating oil.
- Perhaps some reduced risk of certain types of cheating, though under both credits and taxes, emissions must be verified.
- Reduced incentives for companies to delay efficiency improvements prior to the establishment of the baseline if credits are distributed in proportion to past emissions.
- When credits are grandfathered, this puts new or growing companies at a disadvantage relative to more established companies.
- Allows for more centralized handling of acquired gains
- Worth of carbon is stabilized by government regulation rather than market fluctuations. Poor market conditions and weak investor interest have a lessened impact on taxation as opposed to carbon trading.

Benefits of Carbon Trading

Carbon Trading would achieve four goals. First, it will provide signals to consumers about what goods and services are high-carbon ones and should therefore be used more sparingly. Second, it will provide signals to producers about which inputs use more carbon (such as coal and oil) and which use less or none (such as natural gas or nuclear power); thereby inducing firms to substitute low-carbon inputs. Third, it will give market incentives for inventors and innovators to develop and introduce low-carbon products and processes that can replace the current generation of technologies. Fourth, and most important, a high carbon price will economize on the information that is required to do all three of these tasks. Through the market mechanism, a high carbon price will raise the price of products according to their carbon content. Ethical consumers today, hoping to minimize their "carbon footprint" have little chance of making an accurate calculation of the relative carbon use in, say, driving 250 miles as compared with flying 250 miles. A harmonized carbon tax would raise the price of a good proportionately to exactly the amount of CO_2 that is emitted in all the stages of production that are involved in producing that good. If 0.01 of a ton of carbon emissions results from the wheat growing and the milling and the trucking and the baking of a loaf of bread, then a tax of $30 per ton carbon will raise the price of bread by $0.30. The "carbon footprint" is automatically calculated by the price system. Consumers would still not know how much of the price is due to carbon emissions, but they could make their decisions confident that they are paying for the social cost of their carbon footprint.

Conclusion

Though Carbon Trading is definitely a very lucrative proposition for both the buying and selling countries, it is the environment which pays the heaviest price, as the GHG emitting countries cause environmental degradation by polluting it. We live in a world where a balance has to be maintained but in the present situation we are disrupting the balance and the future generations will have to pay a heavy price as they will live in an unhealthy environment. Hence strict laws should be imposed to limit the buying and selling Carbon Credits. Scientists must use their time, money, and all available resources in order to find substitutes for the carbon emitting fuels currently being used so that the environment does not suffer any damage at all. They could use sustainable development programs via renewable or zero carbon emission fuel. Countries need to be the change which they want to see in this world.

REFERENCES

1. Coalition of Environmentally Responsible Economies,(2002) CERES reporting http://www.ceres.org/pdf/CERES_short_form.pdf
2. Deegan, C. and Gordon, B. (1996), "A study of the environmental disclosure practices of Australian Corporations", *Accounting and Business Research*, Vol. 26, No. 3, pp. 187-199.
3. *Environmental Reporting by Indian Corporates*, (2003) Paper presented at International Conference on Environment & Sustainability Leeds, UK.
4. Esty, Daniel and Peter K. Cornelius (2002), *Environmental Performance Measurement*, Oxford University Press.
5. Gray, R. Owen, D. and Adams, C. (1996), *Accounting and accountability, Changes and challenges in corporate social and environmental reporting*, Prentice-Hall, London.
6. Global Compact (2002), http://www.uneptie.org/outreach/compact/about.htm
7. Knoepfel, I., Dow Jones Sustainability Group Index (2001), A Global Benchmark for Corporate Sustainability, Corporate Environmental Strategy Global Reporting Initiative (2002), Sustainability Reporting Guidelines, http://www.globalreporting.org/guidelines.
8. Robertson, D.C. and Nicholson, N. (1996), "Expressions of Corporate Social Responsibility in UK Firms", *Journal of Business Ethics.*
9. Sahay, A. and N.P. Singh (2003). Relationship between Environmental and Financial Performance of Companies (under publication), *Journal of Management Research*, New Delhi.
10. Sahay, A, Environmental Risks and Relevant Insurance Products, (2003), *Paper presented at International Conference on Environment*, World Environment Forum.
11. United Nations (1991), Accounting for environmental protection measures, Paper E/C.10/AC.3/1991/5, United Nations CTC ISAR, New York.

Index